SKIN SECRETS

A guide to healthy skin, hair and nails
for Australian conditions

DR PETER BERGER

Foreword by Professor Albert Kligman,
of the Department of Dermatology, University of Pennsylvania

A Susan Haynes book

Allen & Unwin

For Carolyn

The author and publisher would like to thank Janssen-Cilag Pty Ltd, the distributors of Retin-A in Australia, for all their help with the colour photographs.

First published in 1991

A Susan Haynes book
Allen & Unwin Pty Ltd
8 Napier Street, North Sydney, NSW 2059, Australia

National Library of Australia
Cataloguing-in-publication data:

Berger, Peter.
  Skin secrets.

  Includes index.
  ISBN 1 86373 103 2.

  1. Skin—Care and hygiene. I. Title.

646.72

Set by Midland Typesetters, Maryborough, Victoria.
Printed by Australian Print Group, Maryborough, Victoria.

Contents

Preface

This is a no-nonsense book written on a timely and important subject by a knowledgeable, experienced dermatologist who is also exceedingly frank and critical.

Although the author attacks the cosmetic industry for its excessive claims and absurd promises, the material he presents is truthful, revealing and informative, and may indeed assist the consumer.

Interest in skin-care products, whether drugs or cosmetics, has never been greater. Thousands of products for pampering and improving skin have flooded the market place. A substantial percentage of television commercials and advertisements in magazines and newspapers present the observer with an infinitude of choices which promise health and happiness in a bottle. There are several compelling reasons for this.

People in First World countries have more leisure and money than ever before. They tend to live in sun-worshipping cultures where the tanned look implies social success and status. Of course, this behaviour induces premature ageing of the skin, already detectable by the time of puberty, though not clinically evident. The skin has a long memory and records its earlier injuries relentlessly.

The universal fascination with the subject of skin is thus easily explained. To be sure, skin diseases are numerous and troublesome, which has given rise to the scientific specialty of dermatology, now in the foremost ranks of medicine. However, it is less the diseases of skin which intrigue the average person, but rather, the psychosocial consequences of not having nice skin. Skin resonates deeply in the human soul because of its strong associations with

1

issues that really matter, perhaps more than we care to admit. These have mainly to do with appearance, which seriously affect our self-image, our opportunities for dates and mates, job selection, peer approval, sexual security, feelings of physical well-being and especially the forebodings that come with the passage of time.

The author understands these tensions and contradictions and presents a balanced and realistic point of view. The text deals with the important changes that concern us all, offering sensible and practical advice on how to treat a huge variety of discolourations, growths, defects, disfigurements and lesions which beset the skin.

It should be recognised that we are living in unprecedented times and experiencing a true epidemic of ageing. Since the turn of the century, at least thirty years have been added on average to the lifespan of women living in the industrialised, high-tech world. Skin diseases increase steadily with age. Many persons beyond 65 have three or more conditions which warrant medical attention. No one becomes more beautiful with ageing! Structural deteriorations are inevitable in old age. Still, individuals who assiduously follow the rules of cutaneous hygiene detailed in this book can arrive at an advanced age with remarkably good-looking skin. Moreover, the resources that have been mobilised by dermatologists, cosmetic and plastic surgeons are impressive.

Dr Berger knows what bothers people of all ages and he deals forthrightly with these worries without lapsing into medical jargon. He emphasises everday problems and gives sensible, practical advice regarding prevention and treatment.

Skin Secrets deserves a place on the shelf of the home library, since it contains material for all who want swift and accurate information regarding the travails of the biologic clothing we all wear and want to enjoy.

Professor Albert Kligman
Director of the Aesthetic Division
of the Department of Dermatology,
University of Pennsylvania
School of Medicine

1

More than skin deep

AN INTRODUCTION TO THE SKIN

What is this covering that we call the skin—this amazing envelope that contains some of the most extraordinary mechanisms in the entire body? It is not just the 'gift wrap of life' but an efficient organ of the body which nourishes, guards and protects us 24 hours a day. Yet we take our skin for granted. The skin is surely the most abused organ of the body. We dig, rub and scratch it. We expose it to all the elements, including extremes of heat, cold, sun, wind, rain and snow. In the name of beauty we scrub it, pull it, bend it, paint it and spray it. In the name of health we massage it with oils, cook it in the sauna and bake it in the sun. Yet it survives.

Our skin frequently reflects our underlying state of health. Although most skin diseases are confined to the skin alone, some are associated with internal diseases. In fact the earliest manifestations of diabetes, high cholesterol, thyroid disease, anaemia, AIDS, leukaemia or cancer may all be found in the skin. As a mirror of our emotions the skin is without peer: purple with rage, pale with fright, flushed with pride, blushing with shame and wet with perspiration. All are release mechanisms of the skin that express combinations of inner feelings and skin reactions to tension, anxiety and stress.

The skin also assumes enormous importance in the self-image people have, therefore a major psychological reaction to even a minor skin abnormality is quite common. Because the skin is so easily observed we often seek attention for what to the objective observer may appear rather trivial. Unlike other ailments which are internal, skin conditions are easily monitored. Hence any slight deterioration or improvement may cause a disproportionate reaction. Some people also believe that the skin is the mirror of the soul and may ascribe their diseases or 'visitations' to matters that they may feel guilty about. As a result of these lurking fears and worries, they may require a great deal of explanation and reassurance about what is happening to their skin and why.

There are more than 1000 skin disorders. It is estimated that practically everyone will suffer from at least one of these during their life time. In fact 13 per cent of general practice consultations concern the skin. In spite of this, skin disorders are widely misunderstood. They are the subject of many myths and mysteries which often add greatly to the burden of physical, emotional and social problems already suffered by the patient. A skin disorder can in fact be far more of a handicap than is generally realised. It can affect where you live, how you live, what hobbies you pursue and what sports you can enjoy. It can influence what you eat and wear, which cosmetics and toiletries you can apply, how well you do at school and what sort of job you have. It can affect relations with friends, family and business associates, and even whether you have sex or decide to have children.

It is important for people with a skin condition to understand the nature of the problem as well as what treatment options are available. Understanding how the various creams or tablets should be used, what they actually do and what results you may realistically expect is very useful. It is possible to treat or cope with all conditions of the skin, particularly if you are well informed and avail yourself of the best help available. For those of you without a problem, knowing how to intelligently care for it should enable you to maintain a trouble-free skin. If troubles arise, then being well informed should enable you to recognise the problem early and seek appropriate treatment. Prevention is always preferable to the necessity of having treatment.

Simple and inexpensive skin care is invariably every bit as good as the very complex and usually exorbitantly expensive regimes which are often advertised or recommended. Makers of cosmetics and skin-care products have gone beyond making legitimate promises to beautify skin into a fantasy land of assurances that their new products can actually re-build, re-structure and re-new the skin. Unlike the food or pharmaceutical industry, the cosmetic industry is a secret world, a world most of us only know through the hype image-makers feed to us by means of glossy advertising. We dermatologists are not faultless in this area either. Expert at diagnosing and treating the ills of the skin, most of us ignore the issues of skin care and cosmetics. This has allowed the cosmetic industry to take the lead in 'educating' the public. We have been influenced by fashion and habit into believing that their products are necessary to our way of life—but are they?

Today a youthful appearance is highly prized and sought after. Much research has been devoted to understanding skin ageing and what can be done to retard it. Medical science has in fact kept pace with this growing patient demand to look and feel younger, and there have been significant advances in dermatological treatment and surgery. These now provide the opportunity to have wrinkles smoothed, scars removed and veins eliminated. The choice of methods to help you look young is vast. Some of them are good, some useless and some bad. But the more you know the better your choices will be. Beauty is not, of course, only skin deep, and everyone has the right to both look and feel their best, and to age gracefully.

2

Know your skin

WHAT IS THE SKIN?

The skin is the largest single organ in the human body. At four kilograms and about two square metres, it comprises up to 15 per cent of our total body weight. If more than about one quarter is destroyed, by burns for example, then the body cannot survive. As well as being an extremely waterproof, air-tight, and remarkably supple barrier, the skin is also the living interface between us and our environment.

Indeed, the skin is as important an organ as the heart, lungs or brain. Its principal functions are protection, sensation and heat regulation. All living things, however, are fragile and perishable; everything that functions can break down. The skin is no exception, and being in direct contact with the outside world, it is continuously exposed to all manner of injury. When you consider that it is susceptible to diseases resulting from various internal disorders as well, it is not surprising that its equilibrium, threatened from within and without, is precarious and easily upset. Care is necessary to keep the skin in good condition, and this requires some knowledge of the skin's nature and needs.

The skin is a complicated membrane composed of various layers containing a variety of glands, blood vessels, nerves, lymphatics, muscles and appendages. The most superficial layer is known as the *epidermis*, which is made up of a mosaic of cells varying in thickness from 0.1 millimetre on the eyelid to more than 1.0

millimetre on the sole of the foot. The average thickness would be about that of this page. The deepest cells make up what is known as the basal layer, which is only one cell thick. This is the layer where cell reproduction takes place, and the regrowth of skin occurs. It normally takes about one month for a cell born in the basal layer to be shed as a used and dead cell at the surface. Within this important basal layer of the epidermis are scattered the melanocytes, the important melanin or pigment-forming cells of the skin. These, according to their quantity, dictate the colour of a person's skin.

The outermost layer of the epidermis is known as the *stratum corneum*. It is a tissue-paper-thin layer made up of compacted, lifeless cells which gradually flake off. This layer is a very effective barrier, preventing the loss of tissue fluids and chemicals as well as penetration by dirt, infections and, of course, cosmetic and skin-care products.

Beneath the epidermis is the *dermis*, which is twenty to thirty times thicker than the epidermis and rests upon a thick pad of fatty subcutaneous tissue which acts as a shock absorber and heat insulator. The dermis, which is made up of specialised connective tissue, is extremely important. Broadly speaking, it is composed of two sorts of fibres. The majority are grouped bundles, forming undulating, interlacing bands that are composed of a special protein called collagen. Intermingled with these is a network of other fibres, which are thin, sinuous and elastic, composed of a protein called elastin. These fibres make up only 2 per cent of the connective tissue, the remainder consisting of what is called ground substance. This is the gelatinous material between the fibres that is produced by specific cells known as fibroblasts. It is a unique material comprised of proteins, sugars and electrolytes. The amount of ground substance is greatest in the embryo, and from then on it gradually diminishes until old age, when very little remains. Another important difference between the epidermis and the dermis is their ability to regenerate. Whereas the epidermis renews itself every three to four weeks, the dermis is very slow to regenerate. Therefore, damage to the dermis—mainly by sunlight— is, to all intents and purposes, permanent. On the other hand,

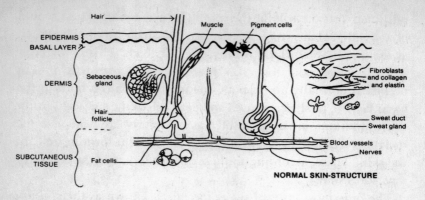

NORMAL SKIN-STRUCTURE

because of the very effective barrier to substances applied to the surface of the stratum corneum, penetration of skin-care products into the dermis is not possible.

The dermis in turn is supported by the *subcutaneous tissue*, which in reality is a specialised layer of the dermis. It is more loosely arranged and has specialised in the formation of fat. The thickness of the subcutaneous tissue varies greatly in different parts of the body and even between the sexes. Its main function is heat insulation and providing support for the various blood and lymphatic vessels that supply the skin with nourishment and drain away waste products. Through it also run the bundles of nerve fibres that form a complex interlacing network throughout the dermis.

There are a number of both essential and non-essential skin appendages. The essential ones include the various glands, and the non-essential ones, the hair and nails. The *sebaceous glands* are a group of specialised cells in the basal layer of the epidermis where sebum is produced. This is an important fatty secretion that is discharged onto the skin surface through a small duct leading into the hair follicle opening. Sebum has a number of functions, one of which is to lightly coat the epidermis with oil, and so help retain moisture in the skin. Another is to improve the pliability of the skin. It also has a mild anti-bacterial and anti-fungal action. Sebaceous glands occur over the whole skin surface, except on the palms of the hands and soles of the feet. They are most numerous on the face and scalp. The activity of these glands varies greatly between individuals and at various ages. During adolescence there is usually an over-production of sebum, resulting in acne, whereas in the elderly there is an under-production, resulting in dry, non-pliable skin.

Apocrine glands are modified sebaceous glands, found mainly in the armpits, genital area, and around the nipples. These are specialised glands that do not function until after puberty. They are stimulated by certain hormonal factors (such as the hormonal changes that occur during menstruation and pregnancy) and emotional factors (such as stress and sexual arousal). Their secretions are responsible for an individual's characteristic odour and may also have some minor lubricating function.

Sweat glands are a specialised group of cells lying in the dermis. These sweat-producing glands are found over the whole skin surface, with considerable regional variation in density of distribution. They are most numerous on the palms, soles, forehead and armpits. The duct of the sweat gland opens on to the skin surface independently of hair and sebaceous gland openings. On the forehead or armpits there are frequently 200–300 sweat glands per square centimetre, and under extreme climatic provocation an individual may produce two litres of sweat per hour. In this way sweat glands are able to flood the skin surface with water, which has a cooling effect, and hence they are very important as part of a heat-exchange mechanism. The closely associated blood vessels dilate or constrict to either dissipate or conserve body heat. This is therefore a very effective thermoregulatory system, one which maintains a constant internal environment, enabling us to escape the rigid climatic limitations imposed upon cold-blooded animals.

WHAT IS HAIR?

Hair follicles are finger-shaped folds of epidermis dipping into the dermis, which are responsible for hair formation. Hair then is a derivative of epidermis, arising from deep within the dermis, and composed of the protein keratin. The most superficial part

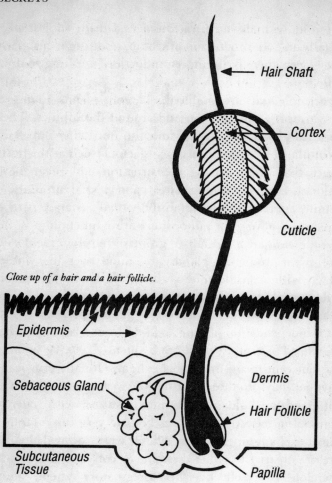

Hair Shaft

Cortex

Cuticle

Close up of a hair and a hair follicle.

Epidermis

Sebaceous Gland

Dermis

Hair Follicle

Subcutaneous Tissue

Papilla

Close up of the cuticle layer.

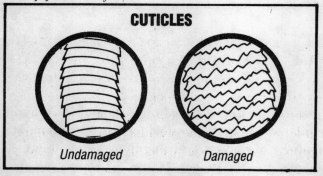

CUTICLES

Undamaged

Damaged

of the follicle forms a duct, in which the hair stands free. Since the sebaceous duct also opens into the follicular duct, the hair shaft emerges through the same pore that secretes the sebum, ensuring its direct lubrication. In the deepest part of the follicle the follicular wall and the hair are fused. This section constitutes its root, the lowest part of which is known as the bulb.

Hair is an extremely complex structure that, broadly speaking, consists of a central cortex surrounded by several protective layers. Hair contains neither nerves nor blood vessels and is therefore a 'dead' structure. There are many different types of hair, which in one form or another cover the entire surface of the skin, excepting the palms and soles. In most areas the hair is short and fine, like that found on a child or the cheeks of a woman, and is known as vellus hair. The longer, broader and usually coloured hair, such as that on the scalp, is known as terminal hair. There is no clear distinction between these types. In fact, the same follicle may produce either type under different conditions. For example, vellus may change to terminal hair on the chin of an adolescent boy, or terminal hair may change to vellus on the scalp of a balding man. The protein-synthesising capacity of this tissue is enormous. When one considers that scalp hair grows at the rate of 0.35 millimetre daily, and that the average number of scalp hairs is about 100 000, this means that individuals produce about 30 metres of hair every day.

WHAT ARE NAILS?

A *nail* consists of the nail plate and the tissues that surround and underlie it. The nail plate has three parts: the matrix, which is concealed within the skin; the fixed portion, which adheres firmly to the nail-bed; and the free edge of the nail. The active growth area is the epidermis of the matrix, which underlies the skin of the nail-fold. Sealing off the potential space between the nail and the nail-fold is the cuticle, which has an important protective function. Under normal conditions, the nail plate is firmly attached

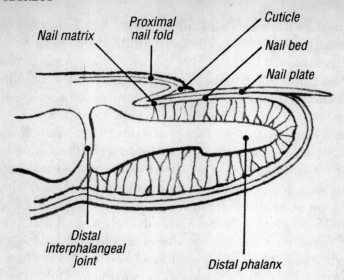

Cross section of the finger, showing the nail plate and surrounding tissues.

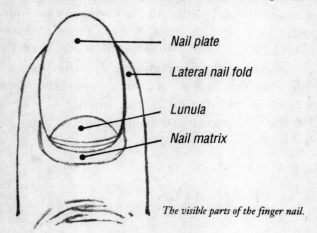

The visible parts of the finger nail.

to the nail-bed. (This may, however, change as a result of various disease processes.) The nail plate exhibits various colour tones ranging from white to pink, which are the result of reflected light from the tissue beneath the colourless nail. The whitish-grey colour of the free edge is due to the air underneath it. Nail is composed of hard keratin, the same protein from which hair is derived. Like hair, the nail plate has no nerves or blood supply, and is a 'dead' structure. Under natural conditions, nails would extend indefinitely unless cut or worn away with use. Unlike hair growth, which is periodic, nail growth is continuous. The daily rate of extension is about one third that of hair, or approximately 0.1 millimetre. It takes about 100 days for the fingernail of a healthy young person to be restored after removal.

SKIN FUNCTIONS

The principal functions of the skin are as follows:

1. It performs an essential *protective role*. Because of its resilience or ability to resume its previous shape after deformation, it can withstand considerable trauma without permanent damage. This mechanical barrier is mainly due to the arrangement and nature of the collagen and elastin fibres in the dermis. It also constitutes an effective barrier to the passage of substances into or out of the skin. This chemical barrier is provided by the layered cells of the epidermis, which impede the loss of water and body salts and prevent the penetration of external substances.

2. The skin is a most effective and essential *sensory organ*. This is because it is richly supplied with nerve endings, which provide an effective sensory defence against potentially harmful stimuli. It also acts as a 'relay station' between external influences and internal organs, via a network of nerve fibres. Of equal importance is its role as an organ of expression: for instance, we may express anxiety by sweating, fear by pallor, anger by redness, pain as a grimace, or happiness with a smile.

3. The skin acts as a remarkable *thermostat*. This is mainly achieved by its blood vessels and sweat glands. The metabolic processes of the body continually produce heat, which must be dissipated to maintain a constant body temperature. Under normal environmental conditions this may be achieved by varying the diameter of the blood vessels in the skin, resulting in changes in the volume of the blood flow. This blood flow can be varied a hundred fold from maximum constriction to

maximum dilation of the vessels. Increased blood flow is accompanied by increased heat loss, whereas a reduced blood flow retains heat.

If, however, blood-flow alterations are insufficient to regulate the body temperature, then the sweat glands are activated. This results from extreme external temperature increases, excessive exertion or the fever accompanying an illness. The sweat bathes the skin and its evaporation causes cooling.

4. The skin plays an active part in the body's *defence against micro-organisms* such as bacteria, fungi and viruses. The surface of the skin is never sterile. It is host to a permanent resident colony of various bacteria which are relatively innocuous. Their presence, however, inhibits the growth of more dangerous organisms on the skin. Further protection is provided by the dryness of the skin's surface. Most organisms are relatively intolerant of dry conditions, much preferring humid or moist environments. The continual shedding of the superficial epidermis also discourages bacterial invaders. Sebum, the oily secretion produced by the active sebaceous glands, contains fatty acids which have a strong anti-bacterial and anti-fungal action. A thin coating of sebum on the skin provides further protection.

5. The skin is an important *barrier against damaging ionising radiation*, such as ultra-violet light. For skin unprotected by hair or clothing, the only significant defence against the destructive effects of UVL is melanin. Without melanin the epidermis would be a thin, transparent membrane, allowing UVL to damage the sensitive structure of the dermis. Melanin is a complicated large protein produced by special cells, melanocytes, in the basal layer. From there it is distributed throughout the epidermis. The amount of melanin in the epidermis governs the colour of a person's skin: the more melanin, the darker the skin colour. There is no difference, though, in the number of melanocytes in white and in black skin. The difference is simply one of activity, reflected in the amount of melanin or pigment these cells produce. Various factors may influence this, including sun exposure, pregnancy, various hormonal disorders, and drugs.

BIRTHMARKS, FRECKLES AND MOLES

Birthmarks, freckles and moles are the result of minor errors that occur in the embryonic development of the various components of the skin. A birthmark is known medically as a *naevus*. This is a better term because many do not become apparent until later in life, although they were programmed to appear before birth. Most of these minor abnormalities are quite harmless, although sometimes cosmetically unacceptable.

A naevus involving blood vessels may vary from a flat, pale pink 'salmon patch' on the face or neck of a newborn infant, to a raised red swelling called a 'strawberry birthmark'. Both usually disappear spontaneously without treatment. The rarer 'port wine stain' usually affects only one side of the face or neck and is permanent.

Freckles are localised patches of overactive pigment-producing cells (melanocytes) that produce pigment in response to stimulation by ultraviolet light more rapidly and effectively than the surrounding melanocytes. They usually first appear at about the age of 5, darken with sun exposure, fade during winter and disappear completely with age.

A naevus involving abnormalities in pigment-cell development is usually known as a mole. Moles are benign growths of the skin. They are uncommon at birth, and their incidence increases throughout childhood, reaching a peak at about puberty, and gradually declining with increasing age. Moles are common in all races and in both sexes. The average number per person in adolescence is about twenty. They frequently increase in number during pregnancy. By the age of 70, however, very few moles remain.

The natural history or evolution of moles is both interesting and important. The earliest or youngest type of mole is the junctional naevus. This is situated completely within the epidermis, at the junction of the epidermis with the dermis. It appears as a flat, brown-black mark without any substance to it. The border is usually irregular, but normal skin markings are visible through it.

By a process of maturation termed 'dropping off', naevus cells begin to appear within the dermis. The mole is then termed a compound naevus. It appears as a raised, brown-black lump with, on occasions, a coarse hair projecting from it. As the mole ages, more and more cells appear in the dermis and eventually, as seen in older people, there is no cell activity in the epidermis. The mole has now developed into an intraepidermal naevus. These naevi appear more regular in outline, frequently raised, but much less pigmented than compound naevi. The maturation process continues and eventually, in old age, there is disintegration of the mole which is replaced by fibrous tissue forming a skin tag. This may simply drop off.

Moles may darken after exposure to the sun, and sometimes during therapy with certain drugs. They also tend to become darker and larger during puberty and pregnancy. However, if there are sudden obvious changes in a mole—for example, in colour, size or shape, or if it bleeds or itches, it is important to consult a dermatologist. If you are uncertain whether a mole has changed in size or shape, then it may be worthwhile marking its outline on tracing paper and retracing it three months later. This will soon alert you to any significant changes.

Certain moles have a higher-than-average risk of becoming cancerous. Moles that are present at birth may fall into this group, especially the large, hairy ones. There is also a special type of mole, known as a 'dysplastic naevus', which may be a warning sign for the risk of developing a melanoma. These are usually larger than the average, with a more irregular border and uneven colouring. Often several moles of this kind may be present. People with this type of mole are thought to be ten times more likely to develop a melanoma than the average individual.

If a mole is subjected to certain stimuli—discussed in Chapter 7—it may not undergo the usual ageing process; instead, at any level of maturation, it may develop into a melanoma. However, only about 25–30 per cent of malignant melanomas arise from a preceding mole.

Any significant—that is, obvious—changes in a mole should be heeded. Some of the changes that may be observed and should arouse suspicion include the following:

- Colour—becoming darker or more variable
- Size—becoming wider or raised
- Shape—becoming asymmetrical, or the border becoming irregular
- Surface—becoming rough or ulcerated
- Sensation—becoming itchy or painful.

There are three common reasons for removing moles:

1. *Prophylactic*: A mole statistically more likely to become malignant.
2. *Diagnostic*: Suspicious changes occurring in a mole.
3. *Cosmetic*: Removal being successful only if the result improves the appearance of the individual.

The choice of technique, discussed in Chapter 7, is therefore important.

THE SKIN DURING PREGNANCY

Pregnancy has a profound hormonal effect on women's bodies. Consequently, changes may occur at all levels of their skin. Some or all of these changes may equally well occur in women taking the oral contraceptive Pill. Being on the Pill is, as far as the hormones are concerned, like being pregnant.

Some of the more common changes are those associated with alterations in the blood vessels. In pregnancy there is an increase in blood flow due to the increased rate of blood formation and the dilation of blood vessels. As a result a woman may develop little blood-vessel enlargements which appear as red spots or as spider-like tracings. These usually occur on the face, chest or hands, and are known as 'spider naevi'. Some women may develop swollen ankles or varicose veins. Many also exhibit very red palms.

Changes in pigmentation are also common. There is a general deepening of colour, particularly in brunettes. These changes are most conspicuous in certain areas, such as the skin about the nipple and the genital area. About 70 per cent of women, especially those with a dark complexion, develop chloasma, the so-called 'mask of pregnancy'. This usually occurs during the second half of pregnancy. It takes the form of irregular areas of brown discolouration in a symmetrical pattern usually found on the forehead, temples and upper lip. These changes can be diminished by adequate sun screening measures, together with the application of such bleaching preparations as hydroquinone creams. Frequently there is an increase in the number of pigmented moles. Similarly, many existing moles, freckles or birthmarks may become darker in colour. These changes need not cause alarm, although if an isolated mole grows rapidly, a doctor should be consulted.

Changes in the pattern of hair growth are also common during pregnancy. Often the appearance of the hair and its rate of growth are improved. This is due to the growing scalp follicles being stimulated to greater activity by hormones. After giving birth there may be a compensatory shedding of hair, which may go on for three to six months. This is due to the hair follicles going into a resting stage. Full recovery usually follows. There may also be an increased growth of facial hair, but frequently this, for some unknown reason, persists after delivery. This hirsutism may also be accompanied by acne.

Fleshy, soft skin tags, or papillomata, may develop in considerable numbers, particularly on the neck, upper chest, and under the breast. They may disappear after delivery; if not, they can be easily removed by diathermy.

Itching is a quite common accompaniment of pregnancy. In fact it may be one of the earliest signs of the condition. Very occasionally it may be associated with a mild dysfunction of the liver or even jaundice. More commonly it is unconnected with liver changes or even a rash, and is simply of nuisance value. The abdomen is mainly affected, and it tends to be worse in the last months of pregnancy. The itching should disappear within a week or two of delivery.

Stretch marks, or striae, also appear on some pregnant women. Similar marks occur on some adolescents, girls being more commonly affected than boys. (Striae will also result from the prolonged use of steroid cream, particularly in the creases.) Both in pregnancy and puberty, these stretch marks are due to excessive adrenal gland activity, together with rapid over-distension of the abdomen, breasts or thighs. Fortunately, after delivery, most cases improve with the passage of time. Otherwise treatment with tretinoin cream can be most effective.

There are a small number of extremely itchy diseases, confined solely to pregnant women. They usually occur towards the end of pregnancy, and invariably disappear after delivery. The commonest type does not affect the foetus, whereas the rarer ones may. Furthermore, some pre-existing skin disorders may be profoundly affected by pregnancy in rather unpredictable ways.

3

Care for your skin

SKIN CARE

Having good skin is largely a matter of luck and genetics. Some people are just born with a lovely complexion, whilst others, no matter how much money and care they lavish on their skins, are never satisfied. Cosmetics certainly have a part to play in skin care, but a much smaller one than the beauty industry would have us believe. A well-balanced diet, only moderate amounts of alcohol, and the avoidance of smoking, do far more good for the skin than anything you can buy in a jar or tube. The amount of care your skin requires depends somewhat on its type. If your skin is oily, such as might be the case if you are an adolescent, it will require different attention from that required for a dry, elderly skin. Similarly, if you are fortunate enough to have inherited an olive or pigmented skin, it will need less care than if you possess a fair skin.

It can be hard to determine whether one's skin is dry or oily, and of course it will vary with the seasons and on different parts of the body, as well as with age. Furthermore, it doesn't really matter all that much, despite what you hear from the beauty 'experts' and skin-care-product manufacturers. If you read the beauty pages of half a dozen magazines, and the advertisements of an equal number of leading companies selling skin-care products, you will be thoroughly confused about how best to look after your skin.

There are certain basic rules which apply to all types of skin.

To begin with, it is important to protect the skin from unnecessary damage. You don't have to spend a great deal of money on expensive products to do this. Weather has an important effect on the skin. Cold weather, and wind, are very harmful because they constrict the blood vessels, thereby impairing the circulation to the skin. Air conditioning, although designed to control humidity and temperature, is often very drying, causing the skin to lose its natural moisture. Humidifiers may help overcome this problem or, alternatively, large shallow bowls of water in the room.

Sunshine, of course, is a major environmental hazard, causing both temporary and permanent damage to the skin, which will be discussed in detail later. However, appropriate protective clothing and adequate sunscreening creams will minimise this damage. It is also important to dry the hands properly after washing or doing even minor kitchen chores. Otherwise, natural skin oils and moisture will be lost from the skin, causing further problems. Using cotton-lined plastic gloves is also helpful.

Naturally, diet plays an important part in all aspects of health. The human body is always changing and repairing itself and these processes depend directly on the quantity and quality of the food consumed. A badly-balanced diet can result, therefore, in skin damage, just as it can result in damage to other organs.

THE SKIN-CARE ROUTINE
Traditionally the basic daily skin routine has consisted of three steps—cleansing, toning and moisturising. Let us deal with these in detail.

1.   Cleansing
All skin types need to be cleansed, for both aesthetic and health reasons. Cleansing removes oily secretions, sweat, skin debris, dirt, cosmetics, and a certain number of bacteria; and can be carried out most quickly, cheaply and effectively with water and soap. Water alone will cleanse skin, but does so more effectively when used with soap: together, they have the effect of emulsifying the debris, dirt and grease on the skin, which can then be more easily removed by subsequent rinsing. The most important part of

cleansing is to use lots of tepid water. Water is effective, abundant, freely available and very cheap. It is an integral part of the human system and therefore compatible with everyone's skin, as well as being very gentle. All soaps—whether transparent or opaque, mild or harsh—are basically made up of animal and vegetable fats, with the more expensive, transparent ones containing extra ingredients such as alcohol, glycerin and sugar. They may also contain less alkali, sweeter perfume or extra lanolin. Transparent soaps are softer and more soluble in water than the opaque ones, and therefore do not last or lather as well. They are frequently promoted as being milder or less drying than other soaps, perhaps because they are less alkaline. Such evaluations, however, tend to be subjective: one's choice of soap might just as well be governed by price and perfume as anything else.

If, however, you have a dry skin, it might be advisable to avoid soap altogether, as it tends to have a drying effect on skin. You will probably find the use of a cleansing cream more suitable.

In addition, dry skin should not be washed as frequently as normal or oily skin. Frequent washing dries the skin by removing normal, oily substances whose purpose it is to keep the skin surface soft and pliable (in fact these oily substances hold a small amount of water within the skin's layers). This dry-skin routine—that is, the avoidance of soap, less frequent washing, and the use of cleansing cream—could also benefit elderly people, those with eczema, or those living in areas of particularly low humidity.

Apart from soap—and indeed, as a less drying alternative to soap—cold cream is one of the best and most popular cleansers. Cold cream is in fact the prototype of all modern cleansing creams. The original cold cream dates back to AD 150, when it was thought to have been discovered by the great Greek physician, Galen. The original formula consisted of a mixture of olive oil, beeswax, water and rose petals. It was termed 'cold cream' because of the cooling effect on the skin when the water evaporated.

Since its discovery, cold cream has undergone numerous formulation changes. Olive oil has been replaced by mineral oils, which do not become rancid, and beeswax has been replaced by more stable synthetic waxes. As a result, we now have a fine, white, glossy cream of firm consistency that spreads easily and cools the skin. The oil and wax provide a cleansing action by liquefying upon contact with the warm skin, and loosening suspended particles of dirt, oily secretions, dead cells, and other material on the skin's surface. They can then be easily removed with a tissue or cloth or, if left on the skin, act as an emollient and relieve excess dryness.

Cleansing creams, in which a variety of oils, waxes and other ingredients such as alcohol may be included, are only variations of the basic cold cream. They are generally thinner and lighter than cold cream, have less 'drag' and feel less oily on the skin. Cleansing lotions and aerosol foams are essentially the same thing in fluid or foam form. Make-up, especially waterproof products such as eye make-up, is best removed with cleansing cream. In most other situations, soap and water are the best combination (except for those with exceptionally dry skin who, as previously mentioned, are better to avoid the use of soap altogether). Some of you may have been mislead by advertisements suggesting that soap alters the skin's naturally slightly acidic property or 'pH', which they suggest diminishes its protective function. However, within half to one hour, the skin's pH reverts back to normal. The reason the cosmetic companies are loath to recommend washing is that they have not yet worked out a way to make a profit from water, although they are now trying to do this by promoting special mineral water and the like from exotic places such as Finland, or remote springs!

At this stage we should consider what is meant by 'a normal skin'. It may be surprising, but there is no accepted definition of what may be termed normal skin. Nevertheless we should not ignore the term: it is in our interests to have some idea of what we should or should not do to attain or retain a 'normal skin'. The popular assumption that a normal skin is one which is neither oily nor dry is meaningless. Typically, a normal skin is firm, because the supporting connective tissue is dense and solid; it is supple, because its elastic fibres are numerous and in good condition; it is matt, because it secretes minimal sebum; it is fine-textured, smooth, without visible pores, and velvety to touch. All this, however, is unattainable—except, perhaps, by a fortunate and healthy prepubertal child.

2. Toning

Toning is a waste of both time and money. The products advocated for this basically consist of water, alcohol and glycerin. They are sometimes called toners, astringents, fresheners or clarifying lotions. A number of claims are made for these products: that they cleanse the skin, refine the texture, shrink pores, control oil and help blemishes. None of these products cause the oil glands to produce less oil, or permanently shrink pores. At best, they may temporarily make pores seem smaller by causing irritation and subsequent swelling around the pores. What these products do best is effectively remove oil and produce a cool, refreshed feeling: nothing that soap and water can't do at a fraction of the cost. Their use is clearly not a necessary part of skin care.

3. Moisturising

This entails the use of creams, oils or lotions to relieve dryness and make the skin feel smoother. Skin varies in its degree of oiliness from person to person, depending on age and the climatic conditions. For example, adolescent skin is oilier than that of the elderly. Also, during the winter, and in air-conditioned buildings, the skin tends to become dried out. Conditioning products, usually called moisturisers or emollients, are designed to prevent these drying processes. They are sometimes described as skin foods providing nourishment for the skin. This, of course, is nonsense. The only nourishment possible is from the inner blood supply— the outer, horny skin layer is inert and lifeless.

These products, whether they be called moisturisers, emollients, nourishing creams, skin food, foundation cream, night cream or 'anti-wrinkle' cream, are all mixtures of an oil and water. Other ingredients are often added to prevent spoilage, to keep the oil and water well mixed, and to provide perfume. Many different kinds of oil, some with fancy-sounding names, are used; there is, however, no evidence that one kind of conditioner is better than another. The various products available may feel, smell and look different, and prices may vary dramatically, but basically they are very similar. All are variations of the formula for old-fashioned cold cream. Although all moisturisers are water in oil, or oil in water emulsions, modern technology has enabled refinements to be made, resulting in the manufacture of many elegant preparations. The final product may be quite greasy, which is then promoted by the cosmetic industry as a 'night' or 'nourishing' cream, or the opposite might be a non-greasy vanishing cream which would be promoted as an 'under-make-up' or 'day' or 'moisturising' cream.

Most moisturising creams act by leaving a thin oily film on the skin which retards the evaporation of moisture from the outer layers. However, it is not possible for externally applied oils or the skin's natural oils to keep the skin hydrated, soft and flexible without the aid of water. This water, however, is the fluid produced by the skin itself as sweat, as well as the fluid emanating from the blood and lymph which surround all the living cells of the body. No drops of water from the outside ever reach the skin's living cells, which is just as well, otherwise we would become waterlogged after a bath or swim! Indeed, loss of water, not oil, from the outer layer of the skin is the basic cause of dryness. Wetting the skin for two or three minutes night and morning is clearly not going to replace the water lost by natural hydration. Even in a temperate climate, invisible perspiration of approximately half a litre daily traverses the skin, quite apart from visible sweat. The only way to prevent the skin from drying out is to trap some of this natural body fluid. This is where the oil in the cream, or the skin's natural oil, are useful. Commercial creams may also contain substances which attract water up from the dermis into the epidermis. Some of these are glycerin, propylene glycol, elastin and Vitamin E. They also act by inhibiting, through their impermeability, the evaporation of water trapped in the superficial skin cells. They also make the skin look and feel soft by cementing down the rough, scaly surface, and smooth it by decreasing the 'drag' felt when touching the skin. They do not penetrate deeply, nor do they prevent wrinkles forming, or help remove them.

The most important question regarding moisturisers is whether you need one. If your skin is oily then you don't require any moisturising, and just because your skin is flaky does not necessarily mean that it is dry. Flaking may also occur with seborrhoeic eczema, a condition frequently associated with oily skin. On the other hand, if your skin is extremely dry then lanolin or petroleum jelly are regarded by many, including Professor Albert Kligman, Director of the Aesthetic Dermatology Division of the Department of Dermatology at the University of Pennsylvania School of Medicine, as the most effective of all moisturisers. The two most important criteria for selecting a moisturising cream are whether it feels good on the skin, and whether it is easily affordable.

WRINKLES

Wrinkles are of enormous concern to most people and are generally misunderstood. This is encouraged by the manufacturers of cosmetic and skin-care products, who promise to erase wrinkles and even sometimes to reverse the ageing process. There are, however, six major factors responsible for wrinkles. By assessing these, a dermatologist can quickly decide whether a facelift is needed to redrape the skin, or an acid peel to resurface the skin, or a collagen implant to recontour the skin.

1. Chronological ageing causes looseness and drooping of the skin. Heredity also plays a role here. Plastic surgery by redraping the skin can prove very effective in correcting this type of wrinkles.

2. Loss of underlying support tissues with age accounts for 'purse string' wrinkles around the mouth, for instance. This is also aggravated by smoking and ill-fitting dentures. Prevention is the key here. Smoking must be avoided, and the teeth kept in good shape. In the future, fat implantation may help to restore the underlying tissues.

3. Sun damage is the most destructive and the most preventable cause of wrinkles. As the sun progressively destroys the upper dermis, the layer becomes thinner, less resilient and more foldable. Imagine folding paper two or three layers thick, compared with thirty to forty layers thick. The thinner paper, corresponding to photo-aged skin, folds or wrinkles very easily. Prevention is as simple as wearing a hat and sunglasses, and applying the highest protection sunscreen available.

4. Movement-related changes. We use our faces continuously, particularly for communication. A raised eyebrow, a frown, a smile, may tell an entire story by itself. Our penalty for that subtle communicative skill is that the skin overlying the muscles responsible for these expressions is folded millions of times in our lifetime. We all smile and express ourselves throughout life, but it is not until significant photo-ageing has occurred that these creases become permanent.

To prevent this is difficult, since it would mean a fairly expressionless face. Our internal feelings would need to be suppressed, much like those of an effective poker player. A more relaxed face may also be obtained through methods including yoga and meditation.

5. Gravity inexorably draws parts of our bodies down with time. This results in jowls, double chins, bags under the eyes and droopy breasts. Plastic surgery can correct these problems by redraping the skin after removing the excess.

6. Sleep creases also eventually become permanent. In children these vertical lines on the face disappear by breakfast. In adults they become permanent. Prevention of these requires either sleeping on your back or using the softest goose-down pillow you can afford.

Having outlined what causes wrinkles and what can be done to minimise them, I must stress that no cosmetic or skin-care preparation or facial yet devised can either prevent them appearing or eliminate them. More of this, and what effective medical or surgical treatments are available, will be discussed in a subsequent chapter.

PORES

Pores are openings on the skin's surface from which hairs may grow and through which oil from oil glands flows to the surface. It is these which give the skin its texture and produce variations between all skins, not only those of humans. You will have noticed the difference between calf and pig skin; similarly, the difference between the skin of young children and adolescents. Pores are small in infancy and childhood because the oil glands are small. At puberty, when the sex hormones begin to flow, the oil glands increase in size dramatically and the pores enlarge to accommodate this increased oil flow. It is widely imagined, thanks to media exposure, that the pores open and close and require 'cleansing'. This is, of course, complete nonsense. Our pores are completely static, and after adolescence never alter in size nor shape, no matter what cosmetic is used. They do not breathe, feed or require 'deep cleansing'. Astringents, which usually contain alcohol, may remove excessive oil and make the pores temporarily less obvious. They may also cause irritation of the surrounding skin, so that it swells slightly around the pores, diminishing their apparent size for a very short time. Nothing, however, can change the number or size of 'enlarged' pores. Pore size is an individual characteristic which no product or treatment can alter.

DRY SKIN
The American public spends $500 million per year on moisturisers alone. Is dry skin an epidemic or is it largely an industry-driven myth?

Skin dryness is a lack of water in the paper-thin, non-living top layer of skin—the stratum corneum. Dryness does not affect the deeper layers—the dermis. The dermis is constantly bathed in tissue fluids and this layer makes up more than 80 per cent of the skin's thickness. Weakening and deterioration of the dermis may cause wrinkles but it is still moist. Wrinkles, therefore, are not a sign of dry skin.

The feeling of tightness or dryness after washing is quite normal. It does not mean that you have dry skin. If it bothers you, though, there are several solutions. Wait 15 minutes and the sensation will pass. Use gentler cleansers. Wash less frequently or apply a light, inexpensive moisturiser after washing. If the feeling persists you may be suffering from seborrhoeic eczema, so check with your physician.

The stratum corneum becomes dry for several reasons. The ability of this layer to hold water varies greatly from individual to individual and the skin oils (sebum) produced by the oil glands vary in amount and composition between individuals. Lack of humidity in the environment plays a major role in surface skin dryness. Also, improper skin cleansing and frequent wetting and drying of the stratum corneum will remove natural skin oils, causing dryness. Finally, a harsh environment, with excessive sun and wind, or air-conditioned buildings, will contribute towards this dryness. So you see, it is quite normal to have a dry skin at times—we all have it. However, skin-care advertisements and beauticians tell everyone they have dry skin and need moisturising. That is not so.

Moisturising the skin is one of the most emotion-packed and misunderstood issues in skin care. Emotions are involved because wrinkling is an obvious sign of our mortality and we want to believe that by using a moisturiser we can prevent, or at least retard, the inevitable process of ageing. The issue is misunderstood because the cosmetic industry wants you to believe that the moisturisers they produce can prevent wrinkling by reducing dry skin. The industry has spent a lot of money brainwashing consumers that dry skin and wrinkles are associated. In reality, they have nothing whatsoever to do with one another. I know this is hard to believe after all you have heard and read. However, dry skin is solely caused by the inability of the surface layers of the skin to retain water. Wrinkling is solely the result of changes in the deeper layers of the skin and cell changes resulting in major structural alterations. This will, of course, happen at the same rate whether you have dry or oily skin. There are no cosmetic creams which will alter the wrinkling process of ageing apart from two notable exceptions—sunscreens or tretinoin cream (Retin-A), which are dealt with in later sections.

HAIR CARE

Humans are hairy animals. An adult has about five million hair follicles, of which 100 000 are on the scalp. Virtually the only areas spared are the palms of the hands, soles of the feet, and lips. Most of the skin surface is covered with short, fair, fine and poorly-developed hair known as vellus hair or 'fuzz'. Certain specific areas, such as the scalp, genital area and armpits, grow coarser, thicker, coloured hair known as terminal hair. There is a marked difference between the hair in different areas of the body, making simple generalisations about hair growth impossible.

Originally, hair had four major functions to fulfil. These were improved sensory awareness; heat regulation; sexual attraction and protection. Of these, only the latter two are relevant today: hair still contributes to sexual attraction, and still protects the nose and eyes.

Hair grows from follicles, which are finger-like indentations of the superficial epidermis and dermis, each of which encloses at its base a small bud of dermis. The hair filament may be regarded almost as a secretion arising from the division of cells surrounding this bud. It is composed of the same type of keratin protein as the skin itself. However, it does not contain nerves, blood vessels or any vital 'sap'. There is therefore no truth to the supposition that dull, lank hair with split ends is due to escaping 'sap', and that singeing the ends will prevent this.

Hair does not grow continuously, but in cycles. All hairs on all parts of the body grow, rest, and fall out according to a cycle which is repeated without interruption throughout life. The duration of various stages in the cycle varies from one part of the body to another, with the scalp growth phase being the longest of all—from three to six years, compared with twenty weeks on the leg. There are three distinct phases of the hair cycle: a prolonged growth phase (anagen); a short transitional phase (catagen); and a longer resting phase (telogen). With the growth of the new hair the old hair is pushed out of the follicle and is shed. At any time in the scalp's cycle there will be anything up to a hundred hairs shed per day. However, as different parts of the scalp will be at different stages in the cycle at any one time, no nett loss is usually detected. Hair grows faster during the summer, and women's hair grows faster than men's, averaging about ten millimetres a month. However, with ageing, the rate of growth slows down.

BASIC HAIR CARE
Because of the cosmetic and sexual importance attributed to hair, and because of the variability of hair growth among individuals,

hair care and cosmetics is a multi-million-dollar business. In the United States, more money is spent annually on cosmetic products for the hair than for all medical research in the country. Unfortunately, the multitudinous preparations and treatments promoted are in the main quite useless.

The first step in basic hair care is to understand something about hair structure. The only growing, or live, portion of the hair is its root or papilla, at the base of the follicle. As soon as the cells that make up hair are produced, they die and become hardened to form the hair shaft. The shaft, like the epidermis, is composed of cells filled with the protein—keratin. This hair shaft gradually moves up the follicle towards the surface of the scalp at a rate of about one centimetre a month. It is lubricated with an oily substance, sebum, secreted by the sebaceous glands which open into the follicle. The hair is composed of three layers: an inner layer, called the medulla; a middle layer, the cortex, which contains the pigments providing hair colour; and an outer layer, called the cuticle.

The cuticle is composed of overlapping cells that resemble roof shingles. When the cuticle layer is intact the hair feels smooth, doesn't tangle easily or break, and looks shiny because light reflects off the smooth surface. If the cuticle becomes damaged from such trauma as incorrect brushing or combing, or as a consequence of hair processing for colouring, bleaching, perming or straightening, some of the cuticular cells will separate and may even tear off. The surface may then become rough and pitted. As a result, the hair will look dull and drab because light is not reflecting evenly off its rough surface. The hair will tangle more easily and the ends may fray and split. (See diagram on p.10.)

Since hair is dead, it cannot repair itself, therefore the damage is permanent. To correct this one must await the appearance of new, undamaged hair growth. No hair product can correct this state of affairs. The aim of basic hair care is therefore to minimise damage to the hair cuticle. This means to treat hair gently and not to abuse it.

HAIR-CARE PRODUCTS

What type of *shampoo* should one use? The requirements of a shampoo are that it should cleanse the hair and scalp, rinse out without difficulty, be non-irritating and cosmetically acceptable, and leave the hair manageable. Often a mild soap will be just as effective in meeting these criteria. A shampoo is basically detergent, water, a fatty material, and possibly some additive. The main ingredient to perform the cleansing function is the detergent. Shampoos marketed for oily hair simply have more detergent and less fatty material than those for dry hair. It is the detergent which loosens the dirt and oil, which are then rinsed off. Soap is also an excellent shampoo if you have soft water in your area. If the water is hard, the minerals interact with the fats in soap to produce an insoluble residue that makes hair look dull unless it is rinsed well.

The shampoo market is very competitive because of poor brand loyalty by customers. So manufacturers keep adding 'special ingredients' to attract our attention. A few years ago it was protein, then balsam and herbs, now various plants such as aloe vera and henna are popular. Who knows what it will be next year? Advertisements claim that many of these natural ingredients bestow special conditioning or rejuvenating properties, but there is no scientific evidence to support such claims. Any other additive in the shampoo ends up down the drain, not on the hair. There are a number of popular additives which may smell nice, look pleasant, or feel good, but which have no significant effect on the hair. Lemon oil, for instance, does not remove oil any better than detergent alone. Egg or egg yolk is merely rinsed out, without providing any additional bonus. Various herbal shampoos possess characteristic odours, but provide no other benefits. Beer makes hair easier to set if used in the final rinse, but mixed in and rinsed off with shampoo it does nothing.

The price you pay for a shampoo is a matter of personal preference. It is not necessary to pay a lot to obtain a good shampoo. With expensive brands, you are often paying for the name and for the advertising costs rather than special shampoo qualities. On the other hand, you may need twice as much of some especially cheap shampoo to adequately wash the hair—particularly if your hair is very long.

Remember, though, to shampoo hair gently. Wet your hair thoroughly with water that is not too hot. Massage the shampoo onto the scalp with the fingertips rather than the nails. Also, rinse the shampoo out thoroughly. Comb wet hair with a wide-tipped, smooth-edged comb with blunt tips. Never brush wet hair because when it's wet it swells and is more fragile, and then may break.

What type of *conditioner* should one use? Unless you have damaged or dry hair, you do not need a conditioner. Conditioners may be useful, but are not essential. Once again, because of the intense competition in the market place, many unrealistic and untrue claims are made for these products. All a conditioner will do—no matter what the price or what the special additive—is provide an anti-static film on the hair shaft. Shampooing decreases the hair's normal oily film, making it dry and the outer cuticle rough, so the hair becomes prone to static electricity, resulting in unmanageable, tangled hair which looks dull. A conditioner simply coats the hair shaft with a thin film that smooths down the roughened cuticular cells and fills in the uneven surface. Consequently, combing and brushing are easier, the hair doesn't tangle as much, and it regains its lustre because light again reflects more evenly off the smooth surface.

You must remember that the hair above the scalp is dead, so cannot be 'fed', 'nourished', 'repaired' or 'strengthened'. Conditioners are not absorbed by the hair, therefore cannot change hair structure, thicken hair, affect hair growth or in any way permanently alter the condition of the hair. Their effects, at best, are temporary and are removed by the next shampooing!

Hair should be conditioned gently. Afterwards, wrap the hair in a towel and pat it dry—don't rub the hair or you will roughen up the cuticular layer or even break fragile hairs. If you use a drier, make sure the temperature is not too high. It is better set on Medium rather than High. Although it may take longer to dry, the lower setting will do less damage to the hair. Similarly, electric curlers should not be used more than two to three times per week, nor a brush with sharp tips. Avoid overuse of bleaches, tints or permanent-waving. Your hair should also be protected from the damaging, drying effects of the sun. After swimming, it is wise to shampoo the hair to remove chlorine and other chemicals and salt water, all of which may produce drying.

HAIR COLOURING

Hair colouring has been practised by both men and women since the days of the Pharaohs. Primarily it is used to conceal the onset of greying, but with the development of more sophisticated and simpler techniques the changing of hair colour now features in the pursuit of fashion. It is estimated that about 50 per cent of women colour their hair. Originally, vegetable dyes such as henna and camomile were mainly used. These were certainly safer than, if not quite as effective as, the newer products. Metallic dyes, sometimes known as 'colour restorers', are mainly used by men to gradually dye grey hair. These dyes are usually made from the salts of lead (resulting in a black colour) or bismuth (resulting in a brown colour). With frequent applications, they gradually change the hair colour. They are relatively easy and safe to use.

The hair dyes most commonly used by women today are the synthetic organic dyes. There are three main types available. The *temporary* ones simply coat the hair shaft with pigment, without penetrating it. They are usually applied as a rinse, and may be removed by shampooing. *Semi-permanent dyes* are the most popular. These penetrate the hair shaft, without drastic pre-treatment, and persist for six to ten shampoos. They are mainly nitro or azo dyes. The *permanent*, or oxidative, dyes are mainly para-phenylenediamine mixed with hydrogen peroxide. Their main advantage is that they last longer and enable hair colour to be lightened. Their main disadvantage is that a significant proportion of people are allergic to them. So prior patch testing is essential.

HAIR CURLING

This is another practice going back many centuries. The Egyptians used to wind the hair on wooden sticks, cover it with mud, and bake it in the sun. Heat-waving processes are still used today but for 'permanent waves' (perms), cold waving techniques are becoming increasingly popular. A perm should maintain the shape of the hair at least through several shampoos; if successful, it may last several months.

Cold waving, being a technique that requires no elaborate

heating or drying equipment, can be done at home; indeed, it has made home permanent waving possible. This process involves wetting the hair with a solution of thioglycolic acid, and then winding it on to rollers; the rollers are left in for between ten and thirty minutes, depending on the type of hair and the desired effect. The hair is then rinsed with a 'neutraliser', usually hydrogen peroxide solution. What basically occurs with a perm is that the hair is chemically changed to a flexible form, like jelly, then shaped as desired and allowed to set or harden for a 'permanent' effect.

Reactions are rather rare considering the widespread use of these products. This may be partly due to the fact that the 'home perm' solutions are weaker than those used in hairdressing salons. The most common reaction is one of irritation, usually caused by carelessly applying the solution or leaving it on the scalp for too long. Damage to the hair is also a frequent outcome. It occurs most commonly with hair that has been too recently waved or bleached, or in normal hair where the solution is insufficiently diluted or is left on for too long. As a result of this damage the hair may become brittle and frizzy, the ends will very likely split, and the hair may even break and fall out. Such hair damage can, however, be largely prevented by following the directions very carefully, and not assuming that different brands can be used in the same manner. Alternatively, ensure that you attend a reputable salon, and make certain that your hair is in good condition before having a perm.

Setting agents, hair lacquers or sprays are mainly based on polyvinyl pyrrolidone or similar polymers. Their effect is short-lived but they are quite safe to use; they do not cause hair damage or dandruff. Occasionally hair sprays may react with some dyes, resulting in discoloured hair.

NAIL CARE

Like hair, nails are derived from the epidermis and consist of dead tissue—the protein, keratin. Keratin contains mainly sulphur in the form of cysteine, which constitutes over 9 per cent, by weight, of the nail. Calcium, however, is present in only negligible quantities, representing approximately 0.25 per cent of the nail's weight.

The nail is formed by special cells found in the lunula, or white half-moon crescent. This extends underneath the skin at the base of the nail. The pink colour of nails is due to blood flowing through the nail-bed beneath the nail. The nail plate itself is white and opaque, like the nail tip extending beyond the end of the finger. Nails grow continuously throughout life, fingernails at the rate of about one centimetre in three months, and toenails at approximately one-third of this rate. Consequently, damaged or diseased toenails may take up to 18 months to grow out. Nails grow faster in warm weather, during pregnancy, and on the right hand if you are right-handed. Growth slows during winter, and with advancing age and illness.

The function of nails appears to be the protection of the ends of the fingers and toes, and the enhancement of the appreciation of fine touch, enabling one to pick up small objects. If the nails are very short, the sensitive skin of the finger tips may become damaged and calloused, and consequently less sensitive to light touch. Nail biters are daily reminded of the inconvenience arising from the loss of this ability.

Careful observation of a person's nails may reveal much about that individual—such things as general health, disease of the skin, temperament, occupation and so forth. Doctors soon learn to recognise the bitten or picked nails of the neurotic and the smooth, well-buffed nails of the scratch addict. A doctor's suspicion of anaemia, certain internal diseases and occasionally even lung cancer may be aroused by careful observation of a person's nails.

General cleanliness is an important part of nail care, to avoid contracting and transmitting infections. Similarly, carefully cut or filed nails will avoid complications such as hang-nail, ingrown nails and paronychia. As a general rule, fingernails should be slightly rounded at their ends, and toenails should be cut straight across.

The care of nails is surrounded by almost as many myths as is hair care.

NAIL COSMETICS

Like hair, nails have become items of cosmetic and sexual significance. Women's nails must be long and strong to be attractive. To be fashionable, their colour must match that of the lipstick or of the clothes. Consequently, there are a multitude of commercial preparations available to help achieve these artificial aims. People throughout the world consume large amounts of gelatin and calcium in the mistaken belief that their nails will become harder, longer and healthier. Unfortunately, as we have seen, calcium is present in only insignificant amounts in nails. Certainly bones and teeth may benefit from the calcium, but not the nails. Gelatin is certainly a protein but it is an extremely poor-quality one which has no effect on keratin, a high-grade protein. Severe protein deficiencies may result in brittle nails; however, as such cases are extremely rare in our society—individuals with this condition would also exhibit thin, brittle hair and body wasting—this deficiency may be virtually dismissed as a likely reason for brittle nails. Another popular misconception is that minor vitamin deficiencies may be a cause of brittle nails—this is not so.

Nail hardeners, developed to prevent nails from chipping, breaking and peeling, are very popular products. They contain formaldehyde, or ingredients that gradually release formaldehyde or acrylic polymers. Reactions to these are unfortunately quite common, and because more and more people are being exposed to this chemical in permanent-press fabrics and in industry, allergies are becoming more frequent. With nails, these reactions may be manifested as discolouration, bleeding under the nail, pain, dryness and, most commonly, lifting and loosening of the nail.

Over-zealous manicuring, particularly pushing back the cuticle, can cause damage to the cuticle in the lunula area. This may result in ridges appearing along or across the nail, which will take months to grow out. Alternatively, infections of the nail surrounds—paronychia—may occur. Special nail creams to 'nourish' nails are no more able to do this than are similar hair- or skin-care products. They may, however, have a temporary beneficial effect on dry cuticles. The most common cause of nail lifting is either repetitive trauma (usually associated with long fingernails); repeated immersion in water; the use of nail hardeners; and, less frequently, some nail diseases.

The use of *nail polishes* and, in particular, of *polish removers*, is thought to contribute significantly to the frequency of nail disorders in women. Brittle and flaking nails especially appear to be at least aggravated by the frequent use of polish removers, which are strong solvents. So it is better to patch up chipped polish than to regularly remove and re-apply it. Lifting of the nails may also occur due to nail polishes or base coats containing certain synthetic resins. Nail discolouration may result from the use of certain nail varnishes, particularly very dark reds and bright pinks. The nails usually become stained a particularly unpleasant nicotine-yellow colour, which cannot be bleached, and will take three to six months to grow out.

There are two types of *artificial nails* currently in vogue. Both may cause significant problems. Pre-formed artificial nails are made from synthetic materials similar to those used in the manufacture of dentures. They are attached to the natural nails with an adhesive, or simply pressed on, and then filed to shape. The adhesive used to attach the nails may cause an allergic reaction to the skin surrounding the nail. The artificial nail itself can cause damage if left on for more than a few days: for instance, the natural nail may soften and lift off because of moisture accumulating under the impermeable plastic.

Artificial nails may also be formed as extensions of the natural nails, using plastic acrylic material. Here a liquid acrylic is mixed with a powder, which thickens, and is then moulded around the natural nail. This hardens rapidly to form an artificial nail which is firmly attached to the natural nail and 'grows with it', lasting for about a month. This product may cause severe (and painful) nail damage. If such damage occurs, the nails will not return to normal for many months, if at all.

4

Skin sense

COSMETICS

Cosmetics fall into two main categories—make-up and skin-care products. The use of well-applied make-up to add colour, accentuate the lips or eyes, conceal blemishes, or relieve dryness or oiliness, is to be commended. These cosmetics help people to both look and feel more attractive, and this is very worthwhile. On the other hand, so-called skin-care products have very little to offer the discerning consumer. This doesn't mean you should now clear out your bathroom cabinets and dressing tables. But I do hope that after reading this section you will feel more confident and knowledgeable and so able to make informed choices. The facts provided here will supply a more balanced picture than that advanced by manufacturers, advertisers and beauty consultants, whose view is usually very biased and commercial.

'INFORMATION'—FACT OR FANTASY?

Until I began to write this book I had no idea of the space devoted to skin and beauty care in women's magazines. Nor did I realise how many magazines and books were published on the subject by beauty 'experts' until I began researching the subject in the major bookshops of London and New York. As an interested, objective but naive reader, I found the information and advice available confusing and often conflicting. Most readers, I felt, would be bewildered by the pseudo-scientific evidence proffered but never explained. The more I read, the more confusing the advantages of the various moisturisers, shampoos, conditioners and rejuvenating creams became. The more material I collected the more I began to realise that consumers were being saturated with non-information. Advertisers and fashion magazines, abetted by the cosmetic industry, had taken the business of cosmetics and beauty and reduced it to clever slogans and pseudo-scientific mumbo-jumbo.

Resisting the myths so skilfully created by a billion-dollar industry is difficult. To be an aware consumer requires unbiased professional information and courage but, as you will see, not necessarily a great deal of money.

There are three major sources of information available to the public concerning the cosmetics industry. The most accessible of these is the articles in fashion magazines. Although these magazines don't actually lie, they don't supply the whole truth either. Beauty editors have been correctly described as 'the eunuchs of the cosmetic industry'. They are fed copy by the public relations agencies employed by the cosmetics industry. Week after week manufacturers' claims, accompanied by glossy photographs, land on the desks of beauty editors around the world. These heavily-biased, subjective blurbs, with the photographs captioned, then appear unedited in the magazines as virtually unpaid advertisements masquerading as independent editorial copy. Often editorial copy is insisted upon as a condition for the placement of lucrative advertisements. It is much cheaper for a magazine to use this PR material than to pay a journalist, photographer and model to supply a similar, and possibly more critical, article. This is why so-called 'beauty editorial' is merely publicity for new products.

Imagine yourself as one of these 'eunuchs' of a major fashion magazine. Your circulation is five million copies monthly. Besides the subscription and newsstand sales, your major source of revenue is your advertisers: the fashion designers, perfume houses, tobacco and liquor companies, and the cosmetic industry. It is virtually inconceivable that you would permit articles to appear in your magazine that clearly disparaged your advertisers. If the advertisers claim to prevent wrinkles, are you going to publish articles which refute this? You can't afford to publish negative commentary, no matter how factual, if it is aimed at the financial cornerstone of your business. This was forcefully brought to my attention following the publication of my first book. Prior to publication, the fashion magazine with Australia's largest circulation expressed interest in serialising the book. However, when it received a copy, it dropped this idea very quickly!

Many consumers accept skin advice from salespeople who have limited and subjective information, and whose only training is in sales technique. A trip to the cosmetic counter of a large department store is a real eye and purse opener. Researching this chapter, I accompanied my wife on several such confusing excursions in Australia, Europe and the USA. I soon discovered that the salespeople are just that: they are there to sell, not to advise. Their brief training gives them little information other than the price and size of their products and, as further inducement, they are often on commission as well. Even when they swap companies these people will swear that whatever product they are selling is the best available. Any slightly in-depth questioning by me usually revealed a total lack of understanding of what the skin does and cannot do, and what the various products can and cannot do. When this was pointed out they would either apologise and explain that this was what they are told to say and 'the company must know', or they would become defiant, grab their manual and try to bamboozle me with 'science'.

We buy about one third of all our cosmetics in department stores from salespeople like these, so it is worth bearing in mind what you are up against. Not only do they aim at selling you a specific product, but preferably a whole skin-care package which might include: cleansers (superficial and deep), toners (fresheners, astringents or pore minimisers), emollients, moisturisers (superficial and deep), masks, packs, balancing cream, vanishing cream, intensive-care cream, anti-wrinkle balm, day and night cream, special eye and neck cream, neutralising milk, nutrient lotions, and so forth!

Because the skin is so visible it has a special significance, with important cosmetic and sexual connotations. However, just because it is a superficial organ doesn't mean that 'surface treatment' is sufficient for its adequate care. Being so visible makes it more prone to varied non-professional treatment than any other organ. Would you allow your cardiovascular system or your gastro-intestinal tract to be looked after by untrained people?

The final source of information we turn to is what you are now reading—the book. The books on the market are also very varied. They fall into three main categories. One is the alternative, or natural, approach to skin care. Here the recipes encourage you to use everything from cucumbers to avocados, plankton to placentas, and aloe vera to mayonnaise. 'Natural' products are enormously popular because they are supposed to be superior to 'synthetic' alternatives. However, all 'natural' products contain synthetic ingredients, whether they be emulsifiers to allow oil and water to mix or preservatives to prevent the products from going rancid. Although strawberry shampoo, orange blossom conditioner, cucumber cleanser and apricot scrubs sound mouth-watering and pure, their only special attribute is their pleasant smell. Furthermore, 'natural' products are not safer than others, since substances in nature are just as capable of producing severe skin allergies. For example tea tree oil, the rhus tree or primula plants can cause severe allergies. The second kind of books are the ones devoted to make-up—what to apply and where and when to apply it. Finally, there is the book written objectively by a professional aimed at informing the reader and consumer, and at separating fact and fantasy. Ideally, the author will be a dermatologist, who is trained and experienced in both the physiology and pathology of the skin. This person knows the type of skin care needed, which products will and will not affect the skin, and how to deal with any diseases which may occur. Such a book should present up-to-date, accurate scientific information so that the consumer can make an informed choice regarding skin-care products and treatments.

THE PSYCHOLOGY AND COST OF COSMETICS

Although it is tempting to dismiss the use of cosmetics as utterly trivial, research shows that an individual's physical appearance has a substantial effect on his or her life. Studies show that attractive people enjoy many advantages, including greater self-confidence and self-esteem, popularity, job success and an ability to move higher on the social scale than their less attractive associates. Most would, I am sure, agree that the skilful use of make-up can improve the appearance of many who are not born naturally beautiful. Make-up enables women to very effectively camouflage their less attractive features and enhance the good ones. Many women put on a daily 'mask' for the world, spending up to half an hour each morning 'putting on their face', and find it inconceivable to venture out without it. The way they arrange their appearance is a projection of the way they want the world to see them. This image does not necessarily reflect the real self, but rather what they wish to project, and indicates the way they would also like to be treated.

The cosmetic industry knows that 25 per cent of the female population is aged between 15 and 20 years, and that by age 13 many girls are beginning to wear make-up regularly. This teenage market is profitable and the youngsters worth exploiting. Despite the recession and youth unemployment, this age group spends a lot of its spare cash on cosmetics and clothes. Perhaps if you can't get a job, and you don't have heavy financial responsibilities, satisfaction can be derived from looking good and possibly then feeling better.

Adult women's sometimes obsessive preoccupation with the way they look extends into surprising areas. For example, a number of important women being interviewed on national television were asked what concerned them most prior to the show. They were unanimous that they were worried more about how they would look than about what they would say. Research has also shown that nearly all women are dissatisfied with their appearance, regardless of their class or level of intelligence, and they worry about improving it. Similarly, the less confident a man or woman feels, the more cosmetic products he or she uses. The more self-assured they feel, the less they use.

The cosmetic industry is one of the most lucrative of all: in Australia it has a turnover of $1.5 billion annually. The skin-cream market alone in Australia and the UK is estimated to be worth $200 million, and in the USA five times as much. The ingredients in a jar, tube or bottle of cosmetic invariably cost less than their packaging, and substantially less than the cost of selling them to us, the consumers. According to figures available in the US, no more than 10 per cent of the cream's cost can be attributed to the product itself; the remaining 90 per cent accounts for the packaging, promotion and sale. This explains why manufacturers are able to sell their products to staff for a few cents when the same products are sold in the shops for several dollars. It also explains why cosmetic companies are so generous with free samples to beauty editors. A favourable mention in an editorial column is considered by the industry to be worth ten times any advertisement they place, because the reader may believe that editorial endorsement denotes some sort of independent assessment, which in fact has not taken place. Hence, the gift amounts to a bribe when you consider the benefit to the company of free publicity in the editorial column.

MAKE-UP PRODUCTS

The history of cosmetics dates back to antiquity. The word itself is derived from the Greek *kosmetikos*, to adorn. There is evidence from Palaeolithic cave paintings of the use of red and yellow ochre for colouring the skin. Queen Mentuhotep, in 3000 BC, owned a small cosmetic chest containing preparations to beautify the eyes and maintain the condition of the hair, as well as deodorant perfumes for the armpits and groin. Ovid, the Roman poet (43 BC–17 AD), lectured the women of Rome on the need to use cosmetics as an essential practice to retain lovers. He also described how the wrinkles of old age may be concealed. In Queen Elizabeth's day, milk baths were the fashion. Turkish ladies of that time were advised to have their skin flamed by a torch held by a eunuch of the harem. Clearly, women for many centuries have been prepared to go to the utmost lengths to improve the appearance of their skin and forestall the inevitable ogre of age. Today, many men also show an interest in skin care and the use of cosmetics.

The basic make-up used is the *foundation cream*. This both protects the skin to some extent from the drying effects of the elements and serves as a base for powder or blusher. As mentioned before, foundation cream is basically a cold cream, which is tinted.

Face powders are a combination of talc, the predominant ingredient, stearates, kaolin, perfume and colouring substances. Talc is a complicated salt of magnesium, whose main characteristic is that it is very easy to spread. Stearates, which are also metallic salts, enable the powder to stick to the skin. Kaolin is a variety of aluminium salt, which acts as an absorbent for perspiration. Compressed powders are the result of combining face powder with binding agents such as gum arabic. Similarly, binding can be attained by the use of a moist sponge applicator to collect and spread the requisite amount of powder on the skin.

Mascara is a make-up used for darkening and thickening eyelashes. The use of *eye-liner pencil*, mascara and *eyeshadow* to highlight the eyes is a popular practice. These products contain various dyes, anti-bacterial agents, resins and bases. Allergies to these are not uncommon, particularly since the skin about the eyes is very thin and sensitive. It is particularly prone to contact dermatitis, being highly sensitive to various cosmetics, especially hair preparations and nail polish.

The colouring of lips for decoration is an age-old custom. *Lipstick* as we know it today is very different from earlier products. Most lipsticks contain oil-wax mixtures, lanolin, staining dye, perfume and colour pigments. Each of these substances may cause an allergic reaction in some users.

Nail polish is essentially a lacquer containing cellulose, nitrate, solvents, resins and colouring agents. The resins which are responsible for the sheen and stickiness are the agents most usually responsible for allergic reactions.

Fragrances may be incorporated in nearly every type of cosmetic and are also, of course, used alone. *Perfume* is created from a chemical formulation of fragrant volatile oils, preservatives and alcohol. The oils are obtained from a variety of sources including spices, flowers and fruits. Many manufacturers now omit fragrances from their products because they may cause allergies in some users.

I am a great advocate for women who wish to use make-up to improve their appearance. One of the joys of life is to see a beautifully groomed and made-up woman. Let's face it, we all admire good skin and bone structure, but few of us have them. Even many fashion models and actors have flaws that they are extremely anxious about. Make-up products enable people to enhance their good features and cover those that are unfashionable or unattractive. Make-up can disguise teenage acne, signs of worry, ill health and, to some degree, age. Overall, it helps people to feel less vulnerable.

SKIN-CARE PRODUCTS AND TREATMENTS

Unfortunately, the cosmetic industry is not satisfied with simply catering to existing fears and anxieties. Marketing machines are not above creating new fears and then claiming to satisfy the needs those fears create. In particular, they tend to exploit one's natural fear of ageing. In so doing they imply that photo-damaged skin can be repaired, which is blatantly untrue, and so prophylaxis— that is, sun protection—is ignored. In this way, the industry first deceives and then exploits the unaware consumer.

Knowing your skin type has been a cornerstone of the cosmetic industry for a long time. In my opinion it is one of the most creative marketing plans of all. It involves developing a need and creating products to supposedly handle that need. The notion revolves around the artificially created definition of what normal skin should be. Then, if your skin type is something other than normal, products will be forthcoming which suggest that they can return your skin to wonderful normality. Some sophisticated companies use computers 'programmed by leading dermatologists' to tell you what should be evident by simply looking into the mirror.

The very idea of normal skin being an attainable goal is

unrealistic since, first, it ignores the dynamics and ever-changing status of everyone's skin. Second, skin type depends on whether you have just cleaned it, and with what; and whether you are feeling well, or maybe menstruating; and what you have just applied to it. Third, the notion of 'skin type' suggests that once typed, it stays that way for a while. However, your skin varies daily, monthly and with the seasons, and of course with emotional changes. Finally, skin type is a subjective evaluation that depends on who makes it. So although 'skin types' exist, they are very variable and therefore not a suitable basis for making skin-care decisions.

Reading cosmetic advertisements gives one the impression that modern skin-care products are the fountain of youth, that they can really change the skin. Whatever the problem, it can surely be cured by these new high-tech scientific products. Also, we tend to believe what we read, imagining that our laws ensure that advertising claims are truthful. We also *want* to believe the advertisers' promises.

Although there is legislation governing truth in advertising, the regulatory bodies do not approve advertisements before you see them. This means the industry can make whatever claims it wishes, within reason, without prior approval. Only when an advertising claim is blatantly false, or when complaints are filed, can action be taken. The ads often sound very technical and scientific, to emphasise the quasi-medicinal qualities of the product. On the other hand, although manufacturers may be unable to produce any evidence to prove their claims, critics cannot always produce evidence disproving the claims. So, by repeated publication, a claim may become part of our growing pseudo-scientific folklore.

Cosmetic companies find themselves in something of a dilemma, for if their products really can drastically alter the nature of skin cells, as they often suggest, then they are technically pharmaceutical drugs. This means they would be controlled by government legislation and subject to very strict independent testing. Drugs are defined as substances that can cure an illness or alter the structure, function or physiology of an organ—in this case, the skin. Cosmetics, on the other hand, are substances sprayed, rubbed, poured, sprinkled or otherwise applied for cleansing, promoting attractiveness or altering the appearance. So we see that if a cosmetic product or ingredient had drug-like effects of any consequence, such as are claimed for the various newer moisturisers and anti-ageing creams, then their sale without legislative approval would be illegal. On the other hand, if the product or ingredient does not have the drug-like effect it claims, then those claims are false!

People have been looking for the fountain of youth since time immemorial, and the emphasis on youth has never been greater than in today's leisure- and youth-oriented society. Because ageing causes such visible changes in the skin, many men and women would like to delay or reverse these changes. Though many cosmetic products on the market claim to do just this, unfortunately none has ever lived up to its claims. Let us consider some of the 'special ingredients' in skin-care products which add 'special' properties to them. Remember, though, that by the time you read this there will be a plethora of new discoveries to tempt you.

Protein

Various proteins are added to many products to make you think they help nourish the skin or hair. Some proteins can form a water-holding gel on the skin's surface and therefore possibly enhance the moisturising properties of a product. Protein molecules are too large to penetrate the epidermis so cannot nourish the skin, and of course hair is dead. Similarly, of course, applying calcium cream will not strengthen bones; and rubbing blood onto the skin will not correct anaemia.

Collagen and elastin

Since the main structural proteins of the dermis are collagen and elastin, and since photo-aged, wrinkled skin has a weak dermis, the hope is that the collagen or elastin in a product will penetrate into and rebuild the dermis. There is some evidence that adding collagen or elastin to a product may improve the moisturising qualities or 'feel' of the product. However, manufacturers imply that collagen or elastin will rejuvenate or replace the damaged collagen or elastin, making the user's skin look younger. This is impossible. Neither of these products, whether cross-linked or not, can penetrate the skin, because their molecules are much too large. Furthermore, these products are either derived from animal sources or are synthetic, so they could never replace the human skin's collagen or elastin.

Vitamin E cream

Vitamin E is currently in vogue for the treatment of various normal and abnormal skin conditions. Like the vitamins A, D and K, it is fat soluble. Only about 400 units of vitamin E per day are required, and these are easily obtained by eating eggs, margarine or vegetable oil. Various claims have been made for vitamin E, in particular that it is capable of the removal of wrinkles and stretch marks, the rapid healing of burns and wounds and the removal of underarm smells; that it can improve sexual potency; and that it can diminish the incidence of heart disease and diabetes. It is used both in capsule and cream form. Vitamin E has become a popular additive in various cosmetic products because of its alleged healing qualities. However, there is no available scientific evidence to support such claims. Vitamin E may be utilised as a preservative or anti-oxidant, which may be useful for the stability of the product, but does nothing useful for the skin. Furthermore, a number of people are acutely allergic to it on the skin, and as a result many preparations have been withdrawn from sale. There is no known reason to use a product containing vitamin E unless you like the product itself. Vitamin E is still considered a vitamin in search of a disease to cure.

Hypo-allergenic products

Some years ago it became evident that cosmetic products were producing allergic reactions in some users. Several manufacturers then began to produce cosmetic lines from which known sensitising agents were excluded. These cosmetics were called 'hypo-allergenic'. Since then the manufacturers of major brands of cosmetics have realised it is in their interest to omit ingredients likely to cause a significant number of allergic reactions among consumers. Thus, at present there is little distinction among established cosmetic products concerning their potential to sensitise. Reactions to cosmetics, while relatively rare, occur with so-called hypo-allergenic cosmetics as well as those not so labelled. To date there is no known method of producing a true non-allergenic cosmetic. Expressions such as 'allergy-tested', 'dermatologist-tested' or 'research has shown . . .', are frequently used in advertising. These claims are meant to lull you into a sense of security. What they don't tell you, though, is who did the testing, how they did it, and how many tests were performed. Without this kind of information you may justifiably remain sceptical.

Liposomes

This is the newest high-tech cosmetic buzz word. A liposome is basically a type of delivery system involving the encapsulation of a cosmetic ingredient into microscopically small droplets. These droplets supposedly have the ability to penetrate further into the stratum corneum, thereby aiding penetration of the ingredient. But remember three things. Molecules of collagen and elastin, for example, are too large to penetrate the skin, so encapsulating them in liposomes can't shrink them. Moreover, ability to penetrate the stratum corneum does not mean the ingredient will penetrate the dermis or be integrated into the cell membrane or be biologically active. Lastly, remember that by law cosmetics may make the skin feel or look prettier but cannot alter the structure, function or physiology.

Hormones

The addition of hormones—usually the female hormone oestrogen—to creams may cause thickening of the thinner skin of elderly females, particularly in the genital area, but not on the face. It is a nice idea to feed the ageing skin the hormones of youth, but it just doesn't work even though it is absorbed. Furthermore, if enough hormone is absorbed through the skin, unwanted side effects on other parts of the body may occur. This makes oestrogen by definition a drug, and not a cosmetic.

Some of the most expensive skin-care products come from elite-sounding Swiss or French institutions that provide 'cellular' extracts from monkey embryos and sheep placentas. This, of course, is the ultimate or the elixir of life. Unfortunately, there is no evidence that they have any beneficial effect whatsoever. Their exorbitant price is part of the marketing strategy. Anything that is so expensive must be good.

By now it should be clear that my message is: 'if something sounds too good to be true, it probably is not true'. This also applies very much to facials.

Facials

Skin-care salons, like hairdressing salons, vary greatly in their level of expertise; what they offer; and how much they cost. Each has its own regimen for skin assessment, cleansing, nourishing, toning, stimulating and rejuvenating, as well as cosmetic recommendation. A facial may last anywhere between half an hour and two hours, and cost from $30 to $100, not including the range of cosmetics you end up buying, which may cost several hundred dollars more.

At the initial visit you are given a skin analysis and told what 'skin type' you have. The only problem here is that, as we have seen, there is no such thing as a specific and exclusive 'skin type', and the usual salon definition of normal tends to exclude most of the human race. Also, if you visit a number of different salons you are very likely to receive very different 'diagnoses'.

Salons have also entered the same high-tech age as cosmetics. You may be either impressed or intimidated by the array of machines and products available. Treatments you may undergo include cathiodermie, biopeeling, electrotherapy or oxygenation, to name a few. Deep cleansing is one of the favourites, either using steam or various masks. Unfortunately, pores cannot be opened or closed, and nothing reaches the bottom of pores to clean them anyway. Furthermore, whiteheads, pimples or acne cysts no longer possess any pore openings to the surface to allow trapped material to escape. As a result, facials invariably aggravate acne-prone skin. Even blackheads, which may be removed by such therapy, quickly re-form, and excessive force with an extractor may result in scarring. Masks, like astringents, brushes, vigorous massaging or vibrating, slightly irritate the skin, resulting in slight swelling. It is precisely this swelling that gives that *temporary* apparently 'tighter pored', healthier, 'glowing' look. Electrical stimulation of the skin also results in temporary swelling, with apparent 'smoothing' of wrinkles. It is one of the ironies of having facials that, after going to such trouble cleansing and treating the skin, most salons can't wait to cover it all up again with masses of make-up.

Nevertheless, there are two real benefits you may receive from having a facial treatment. The first of these is a feeling of being pampered, and relaxing. There is nothing wrong with this, especially since stress shows on the face. Tiny muscles tighten and accentuate existing facial wrinkles. Following treatment these lines will ease for at least two to three hours. The other advantage is that the facial therapist should be able to show you how best to enhance your appearance or cover blemishes with make-up. However, beware of purchasing expensive, ineffective skin-care products. Remember, they are cosmetics, not drugs. Most of us are very tempted to buy dreams and promises. Unfortunately, these cannot be packaged in jars. Those of you with a skin disease should definitely avoid having facials, as these may either aggravate your condition or delay your seeking expert medical advice. For those of you with problem-free skin and ample finances and time, facials can be a most relaxing and self-indulgent experience. Please do not expect more, or you may be disappointed.

It can thus be seen that a considerable number of untested and/or misleading claims are made in the field of skin-care products. The external application of any nutrient, vitamin or other exotic substance will have no effect on the basic nature of a person's skin. That is, the skin cannot be fed or nourished by any known cosmetic. The realistic person will accept the limitations of cosmetics as well as their benefits. Cosmetics help people to look and feel more attractive, but they accomplish this solely through such properties as colour, fragrance and local physical action. They cannot, to date, rejuvenate or change the basic nature of the skin.

5

Cherish your skin

AGEING SKIN

When we talk about ageing skin, it is very important to distinguish changes that occur simply with the passage of time from those that are the consequences of sun exposure. Many changes, such as wrinkling, freckling, 'broken capillaries', and that 'leathery look', are the result of what we now term photo-ageing, or chronic sun damage. Skin changes that are attributable to true chronological ageing include: increased dryness, decreased sweating, changes in hair growth and in facial and body contours. These differences are summarised in the table on p. 55.

As the skin ages, the rate of cell production and turnover slows down and cell repair is less effective. The epidermis—the outer layer of the skin—becomes thinner, whereas the stratum corneum—the outermost layer of the epidermis—actually becomes thicker. As a result it dries out, cracks, and develops a rough, scaly surface. This thinned epidermis, of course, bends much more easily, therefore allowing wrinkling. Also, once thinned, the epidermis admits even more sunlight, causing even more thinning and wrinkling, thus perpetuating the problem. The normal skin of an infant is a beautifully organised structure that has been compared to a carefully arranged, perfectly stacked and well-cemented brick wall. Sun damage, though, causes chaos in those cells, as if they had been hit by a severe storm. The cells, or bricks, become completely disrupted and begin to look like a dilapidated brick wall. Not only do the cells become disordered, but so do the nuclei, the control centre that regulates cell growth. Because of this DNA disruption, induced by sunlight, mistakes are made in the copying process as the cells reproduce. They then begin to resemble cancer cells. Eventually, at sites of photo-ageing, benign or malignant growths will appear.

Skin colour also changes. Pigment cells usually become less active as the blood supply decreases, so the skin looks more sallow. Sometimes they become completely inactive, leaving small white spots. On the other hand, particularly in areas of chronic sun damage—photo-ageing—the pigment cells become overactive, producing blotches of excess pigmentation. These are often erroneously called age spots, senile freckles or liver spots! They are amongst the classical signs of photo-ageing and as such might be better called premature age spots, to help people understand that they are sun, not age, related.

Changes in facial contour occur because of some loss of fat and redistribution of existing fat in the subcutaneous layer of the skin. This is thought to be due to hormonal adjustments. Changes in nerve endings may cause the skin to be less sensitive to temperature and even pain. Perhaps this is why the elderly tolerate injections and other minor procedures such as cryotherapy so well. Scars also tend to be finer and more cosmetically acceptable. Hair on the face, and in the nose and ears, becomes coarser and more obvious, whilst scalp and body hair diminishes and, because of less active pigmentation, turns white. Sweat and oil glands are less active and so the skin becomes drier, and consequently the elderly are often troubled by itching. The skin of the elderly is more easily injured and heals more slowly following injury, and minimal bumping results in considerable bruising. This occurs particularly on the arms and backs of the hands—sites of chronic sun damage, that is, photo-ageing.

With chronological ageing, the lower layers of the skin—the dermis—also become thinner. Photo-ageing is the result of sun penetrating to these lower layers, where it damages the supportive structural proteins—collagen and elastin. Consequently the skin loses its elasticity and firmness, so it sags and wrinkles.

Collagen is the major strucural protein in the dermis providing support for the overlying epidermis. It, together with its protein partner elastin, constitutes the bulk of the dermis. Normal undamaged strands of collagen look like ropes, arranged in bundles in an interlocking network. Elastin is also a tough protein that looks like fine elastic bands arranged in a delicate branching network. With accumulated solar damage the orderly bundles of collagen disintegrate into useless clumps, and the delicate elastin fibres condense into a jelly-like substance. Gradually, the supporting framework of the skin becomes re-absorbed and slowly disappears, leaving the skin thin, loose and worn out! This can be easily demonstrated by what I term the 'pinch test'. If you pinch up the skin on the back of the hand you can assess a person's age, or more accurately photo-age, by how quickly or slowly it snaps back. Fast is young or protected, slow is old or unprotected.

Ageing

Chronological (inevitable)	Photo-ageing (preventable)
• Roughness	• Roughness
• Looseness	• Looseness
• Wrinkles	• More, and deeper, wrinkles
• Benign growths	• Coarseness
	• Sallowness
	• Irregular pigmentation
	• Broken blood vessels
	• Lentigines
	• Benign growths
	• Premalignant growths
	• Malignant growths

With continued chronological and photo-ageing the skin may become host to a large number, and variety, of growths and colour changes. The majority of these will be benign but often cosmetically unacceptable. They may include the following:

'Broken capillaries' (telangiectasia): These are in fact not broken at all, they are simply more visible because the skin has become thinner and the blood vessel more dilated and therefore much more prominent. They mainly affect the face because it is always exposed to the elements—mainly sun.

'Skin tags' (acrochordons): These are small, flesh-coloured growths that often hang on fine stalks. They are more common on the sides of the neck, eyelids, or in creases.

'Senile warts' (seborrhoeic keratoses): These are the most common skin growths occurring in middle to late life. There is generally a family history for their development. The keratoses are usually brown overgrowths of varying size and number. They have a greasy or crumbly, 'stuck on' appearance in varying shades of brown. They are definitely not warts, nor associated with senility!

'Liver spots' (solar lentigines): These spots only appear on sun damaged skin. They are not the same as freckles (ephelides), which are common in childhood and tend to diminish in adulthood. They do, however, look like large, more irregular and darker, freckles, but are evenly coloured throughout. They are caused by overactive pigment cells.

'Overgrown oil glands' (sebaceous adenomata): These glands are only found on the face, and usually several are present. They appear as small, round, lobulated, yellowish lumps under the skin. It is important to recognise these harmless lumps because they can closely resemble a small skin cancer, known as a BCC.

'Blackheads and whiteheads' (small sebaceous cysts): These are quite common on sun-damaged skin. These look similar to those associated with adolescent acne. However, in this case they are unrelated to acne or, of course, lack of adequate cleansing. Simply, the pores become narrower with solar damage and eventually then they block and small cysts form.

One of the facts of life seems to be that we are genetically pre-programmed for our skin's support systems to gradually break down as we age. At some point the collagen and elastin gets tired of holding things together and therefore laugh lines, furrowed brows, jowls, flabby necks and drooping eyelids, not to mention breasts, stomach and buttocks, all appear to some degree. Also, with the passage of time our bones, fat and muscles gradually shrink and the skin tends to stretch. Together, these changes alter 'the fit' of our skin, contributing to the development of sagging and wrinkling.

However, radiation in accumulating amounts rapidly increases the destruction of the collagen and elastin, making the supportive layers of the skin thinner and weaker earlier. On the skin's surface the opposite happens. Here, radiation causes this layer to become thicker, creating furrowed ridges that overlap and look heavy. Eventually we are confronted with the 'leathery look', interspersed with telangiectasia and blotchy pigmentation indicative of photo-damaged skin. All this can be well demonstrated by what I term the 'buttock test'. Take a good look at yourself in a full-length mirror. First examine the skin on your face, neck and hands, and compare this with your buttocks. Look in particular at the skin tone, colour, elasticity ('pinch test') and texture. Chronologically it's all the same age, but how does it shape up for its photo-age?

RETAINING A YOUTHFUL APPEARANCE

At one time, particularly in ancient cultures, the outward indications of ageing were considered signs of wisdom, experience and distinction. Over the past several centuries, however, particularly in Western cultures, this philosophy has slowly changed. Today, a youthful appearance is highly prized and sought after. Consumers spend many millions of dollars annually on skin-care products that deceptively claim to be able to achieve this goal. Medical science has kept pace with this growing demand to look and feel younger. Research into ageing is a popular new field, and great advances in cosmetic, dermatological and plastic procedures have occurred.

Before you start on your "perfect tan" take a good look at a prune

Three of the simplest and most effective methods available to retard skin ageing are available without prescription. These are:
1. Sun protection
2. Tretinoin cream (Retin-A)
3. A healthy lifestyle.

1. SKIN PROTECTION

The effects of prolonged sun exposure will occur simply by living in countries with vast amounts of natural sunlight, such as Australia. Exposure occurs daily on the face, neck and hands, and frequently also the legs. Actual sun bathing is not required. Simply walking in the streets, hanging out the washing, playing at school, and working the land are all sufficient. The effect of this sunlight on the skin is cumulative. That is, each exposure does some damage, and the effects gradually become irreversible, with permanent damage occurring. Microscopic studies have shown that by 20 years of age, over 80 per cent of individuals have some evidence of permanent skin damage. By the age of 40, all individuals examined showed signs of permanent damage in sun-exposed areas.

Sun exposure, and therefore the beginning of cumulative radiation damage, commences during early childhood, when the skin is at its most susceptible. Consequently, the protection of children is vital to prevent premature ageing and skin cancer in adults. This protection, however, must continue during adulthood as well. According to research in the USA, 75 per cent of the lifetime dose of UV radiation is accumulated before the age of 20. To quote Professor Albert Kligman of the Aesthetic Dermatology Division of the Department of Dermatology at the University of Pennsylvania School of Medicine: 'Every Caucasian woman past the age of 15 has severe structural changes in her facial skin'. In Australia, 90 per cent of individuals over the age of 45 have visible evidence of severe photo-damage. Unfortunately, the skin lacks adequate defence mechanisms against the damaging effects of ultraviolet and infrared radiation and this is why it must be protected. Natural protection would be best. This means avoiding sun exposure when it is at its strongest, between 10 am and 2 pm. It is estimated that avoiding exposure during these four hours would reduce the total sunlight received by about 60 per cent. Alternately, if you are outdoors you should seek out shade either in the form of buildings, trees, umbrellas or hats. Broad-brimmed or Legionnaire-style hats are best.

A more convenient form of protection is afforded by chemical sun screens. A sun screen is a product intended for application to the skin to reduce the intensity of UV radiation reaching it. It should be easy to apply, form a thin, invisible film and resist removal by perspiration and swimming. Most importantly, it should be a broad-spectrum screen, which absorbs both UVA and UVB radiation. It used to be thought that UVB radiation was the only wavelength to cause burning and permanent sun damage, so these wavelengths were the first to be screened out. However, it is now clear that both UVA and UVB cause premature skin ageing and skin cancer. There is even some evidence that long-range infrared radiation (IR) may also be harmful to the skin. It is thought that, by heating the skin, the IR rays allow more damage to be done by the UV rays.

The majority of lifetime UV exposure occurs during multiple, brief, unintentional exposures, therefore daily sun protection is essential. Sun screens should be applied to dry skin, preferably a quarter to half an hour before sun exposure, and be re-applied if sweating is profuse or swimming frequent. They are classified according to the amount and range of the UV radiation they absorb. The sun protection factor (SPF) is a measure of their ability to absorb UVB. It is a multiple of the amount of time taken before a person's unprotected skin will burn. Studies have shown that in Australia at midday, in summer, unprotected fair skin will burn, on average, after twelve minutes. Under similar circumstances in the USA, the average time is twenty minutes. So using an SPF 15 sun screen will allow the average Australian 180 minutes' sun exposure before burning. Some products also contain substances which reflect the radiation, which may also be beneficial.

Currently, most sun screens use Padimate-O, Cinnamates and Parsol to filter UVB, and Benzophenones and Parsol to filter UVA, and Titanium Dioxide to reflect UVA, UVB and IR. Many bases are available, including various creams, lotions and milks. However, an alcohol base appears to be particularly effective because, when applied to the skin, the alcohol evaporates, leaving a high concentration of UV filter. It also is non-greasy, and doesn't run into the eyes with sweating. A disadvantage may be its tendency to dry the skin temporarily. One must always use a sun screen with a minimum of SPF 15, because anything less will not provide a broad-spectrum screen—that is, will not cut out both UVA and UVB radiation. This means that although you may not burn you will still be accumulating radiation damage that causes premature ageing and cancer. Although some screens may claim to have an SPF of up to 40, this has only a marginal effect on their screening capability. An SPF 15 product filters out 93 per cent of UVB, wheras

SPF 30 only increases this to 96 per cent.

Neither sunburn nor tanning is necessary to develop premature ageing or skin cancer. You only need to stay in the sun a fraction of the time it takes to get sunburned to get a dose of UVA and UVB which, when accumulated gradually over years, will permanently damage skin cells. It is possible to tan whilst wearing a sun screen, although it will not be as dark a tan or as fast as without a sun screen. Remember, however, that a tan does not protect the skin. A tan is the skin's response to UV injury, and therefore a sign that damage has already occurred.

The only totally effective method of avoiding photo-ageing would be to completely avoid the sun. A more satisfactory solution is to apply an SPF 15, water resistant, broad-spectrum sun screen preparation every morning as part of one's daily grooming, along with such routines as hair combing and teeth cleaning. This is necessary in Australia, and countries with a similar climate, because of the cumulative effect of the sun from birth onwards. It is the number of hours of exposure to the sun, rather than the intensity of any single exposure, that is the crucial factor with regard to the onset of premature ageing and the formation of skin cancer.

Western society's desire to follow the trend and seek a tan, no matter what the cost to the pocket or the skin, often outweighs the advice given about the dangers of prolonged exposure. Warnings of premature wrinkling and skin cancer are hard to take seriously when you are a teenager, as the effects do not become apparent for ten to thirty years. There is obviously a need to educate young people, and it is to be hoped there will come a day when instead of brown being beautiful, white will be wonderful, or indeed 'pale will be perfect'.

2. TRETINOIN CREAM (RETIN-A)

Tretinoin (retinoic acid) cream is a vitamin A derivative that was developed over twenty years ago for the treatment of acne. Several important derivatives of vitamin A are used by dermatologists. These include Isotretinoin for the treatment of severe cystic acne, and Etretinate for severe psoriasis. It has been found that these drugs have a profound effect on cell differentiation. This means that cells that have become undifferentiated, or disorganised, can be reorganised again. In acne treatment, what this means is that the disorganised cells in the pores that cause blockages, or blackheads, can be reorganised so that the blackhead dissolves and clears. Similarly, in psoriasis the abnormally disorganised or undifferentiated cells will become reorganised or differentiated again, and the skin will return to normal.

Because oral vitamin A can be very toxic and may cause birth defects, a search ensued for a safe cream that could be applied rather than taken. This is Tretinoin. Professor Albert Kligman, the famous guru of skin ageing, and his co-workers, discovered this drug in 1969. Gradually their patients noticed a marked improvement in the appearance of their skin, so they began studying this drug in detail on hairless mice, and then humans.

How does it work?
It has been found that tretinoin has some remarkable effects on the structure of skin:

• It increases blood flow and new blood vessel formation. This improved skin circulation is essential for a healthier skin.

- Cell differentiation is improved. This means the epidermal 'brick wall' is rebuilt, because the cells become uniform and well-ordered again. As a consequence, the epidermis thickens up once more.
- Dermal restructuring occurs, with increased production of new collagen just beneath the epidermis. The number of small fibrils that anchor the epidermis to the dermis also doubles after only four months' treatment with tretinoin.
- The number of pigment-producing cells is also reduced, with clearing of mottled skin discolouration.
- Eventually the uneven dry patches disappear because of gradual exfoliation (peeling) of the surface, resulting in a smoother skin.

What does it do?

It is not a miracle in a tube, or the fountain of youth, nor a substitute for good skin care. However, after four to six months of regular use most people notice the following changes:

- There are fewer fine wrinkles, particularly around the eyes and corners of the mouth.
- Skin colour has improved from a sallow appearance to a rosy glow.
- The skin becomes firmer.
- Fewer lumps are apparent and the skin feels smoother.
- Finally, the pigmented patches and sun-induced freckles have faded.

What side effects could there be?

The main adverse effects of Tretinoin appear early and gradually improve as treatment is continued. These include mild redness, dryness and itching of the skin. Occasionally the skin may become a little more sensitive to sunlight, but this also improves with usage. Very early research, which was never confirmed, showed that in experiments on hairless, albino mice, some developed skin tumours; but in twenty years of human experience there has been no such increase in the incidence of skin cancer. The opposite is, in fact, true. Furthermore, because of the improved cell differentiation with the vitamin A derivatives, Tretinoin is now being used for the treatment of both premalignant and malignant lesions, including skin cancer! It has not been shown to have been absorbed into the blood stream, and birth defects from the cream are unknown.

Who should use it?

Although this drug only has government approval for the treatment of acne, this doesn't necessarily mean it cannot be used for other conditions. The decision to use Tretinoin must remain a judgement made by you, the consumer, and not a bureaucrat. To make this decision you should be well informed and preferably have also discussed the matter with a dermatologist. Unlike in Australia, Tretinoin is only available on prescription in the USA, which ensures that it is not regarded as a cosmetic, and appropriate advice on exactly how it is to be used can be given. Although Tretinoin will reverse many of the changes associated with photo-ageing, it is also very effective in prophylaxis—that is, prevention. It is probably advisable to start using it in conjunction with sunscreening measures in your mid 20s, to slow down the progression of photo-ageing.

How should it be used?

Tretinoin cream should be used daily in the following manner:

* Apply the cream only at night, and to the entire face.
* Always use an SPF 15 sun screen during the day.
* Avoid exposure to the sun.
* Use a simple, inexpensive moisturiser whenever necessary, but not at night with Tretinoin. Professor Albert Kligman recommends Vaseline (petroleum jelly) as the best moisturiser.
* Wash with mild soap and water, not more than twice daily, and pat dry. Apply Tretinoin on dry skin.
* Begin the treatment slowly. On the first night leave the cream on for five minutes only before washing it off. The next night

it may be left on for fifteen minutes. Thereafter you may increase the treatment periods by thirty-minute intervals up to two hours. If, after this time, there is no marked redness, dryness or itching the following day, the cream may be left on overnight.

- Avoid accumulation of excess cream in the corners of the eyes, mouth and nose.
- Do not use soaps, shampoos, astringents and other skin preparations containing menthol, lime or alcohol. Do not take vitamin A orally.

You must expect some redness, irritation and dryness initially; some skin types may be too sensitive to use Tretinoin. A thirty-gram tube should last you about a month if used on the face and neck. Improvement will take a minimum of three months to become apparent. Tretinoin may also be used on the arms and hands, but improvement will be slower in these areas. After one year's regular use, some dermatologists believe that three months' use annually will maintain the drug's effect.

It must be emphasised that Tretinoin is a medicament, not a cosmetic. In the USA it is a prescription drug, whereas in Australia it is not. Nevertheless, I believe it should only be used under medical supervision.

What about the future?

The reversal of skin changes related to photo-ageing results in a much improved appearance, with concomitant improvement in our sense of well-being. Once they are aware of the association between sun exposure and skin ageing, most individuals reduce their exposure to the sun significantly. As a result of this, and the application of Tretinoin, they develop fewer premalignant and malignant growths as well as looking years younger. We have yet to fully understand how these vitamin A derivatives work so that we can maximise their potential. Also, we must develop an appropriate maintenance regimen and learn when we can safely stop treatment. A search for other derivatives of vitamin A that may be equally, or more, successful is, of course, actively under way.

3. A HEALTHY LIFESTYLE

'To look good, you have to feel good'! How often have we heard this truism? A healthy, stress-free person certainly seems to radiate a sense of well-being and often looks much younger than his or her years. A healthy lifestyle includes a sensible, well-balanced *diet*, adequate *exercise*, and a *positive mental attitude*.

Diet: Sensible food habits are an important lifestyle factor. To achieve a nutritious diet we must choose a variety of foods from five basic food groups:

1. Bread and cereals—for energy and fibre.
2. Vegetables and fruit—for vitamins and minerals.
3. Meat or meat alternatives—for protein.
4. Milk and milk products—for calcium.
5. Butter or margarine—for vitamin A and energy.

We must avoid overeating and, in particular, limit our intake of fat and sugar. It is also important to eat less salt and to drink no more than twenty-eight glasses of alcohol per week for men, and half that amount for women.

Exercise: A fit-looking, physically flexible and agile person obviously looks younger than an obese, sluggish individual. Physically active people benefit in many ways. Not only does exercise improve the skin, it also lowers the risk of coronary artery disease, as well as reducing tension or stress. You should select an exercise you enjoy, such as running, swimming, cycling or walking. It should be pursued for at least twenty minutes, three times a week, at a level associated with some breathlessness. This type of aerobic exercise, as it is called, can be commenced quite gradually but should be progressively increased in intensity and frequency to have the desired effect.

A positive mental attitude: Our emotional state has a profound effect on the appearance of our skin. The first signs of ageing are often the wrinkles induced by stress, sadness or depression. Just look at the way presidents or prime ministers age whilst in office, and how quickly they recover when they leave the 'rat race'! There

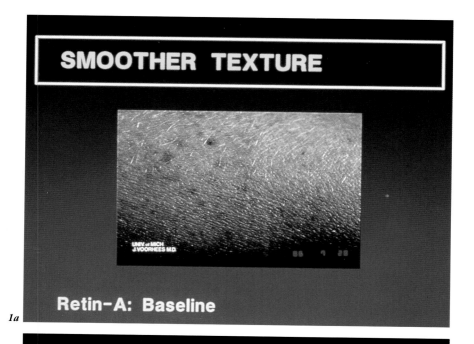

Retin-A: Baseline

1a

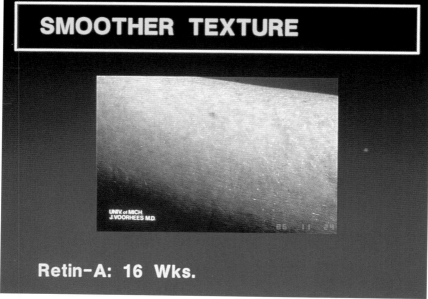

Retin-A: 16 Wks.

1b

1a and *b*. After applying Tretinoin (Retin-A) cream for 16 weeks the skin is smoother and there are fewer sun-induced freckles.

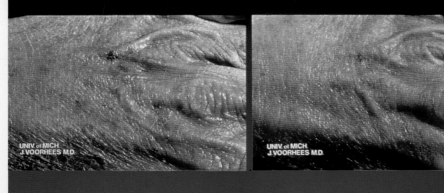

PREMALIGNANT CHANGES

UNIV. of MICH.
J. VOORHEES M.D.

UNIV. of MICH.
J. VOORHEES M.D.

Retin-A: Baseline   Retin-A: 16 Wks.

2

2. After applying Tretinoin (Retin-A) cream for 16 weeks the skin is firmer and pre-cancerous changes are diminished.

3a and b. After applying Tretinoin (Retin-A) cream for 16 weeks the skin colour is improved and there is less fine wrinkling.

FINE WRINKLING

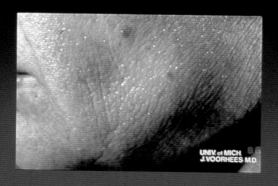

UNIV. of MICH.
J. VOORHEES M.D.

Retin-A: Baseline

3a

FINE WRINKLING

UNIV. of MICH.
J. VOORHEES M.D.

Retin-A: 16 Wks.

3b

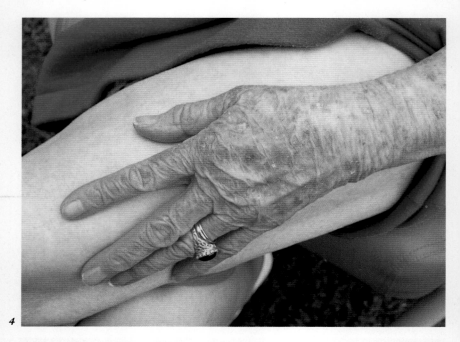

4. *This photograph illustrates the difference between the photoaged skin of the more exposed hands and forearm compared with the skin of the relatively unexposed thigh, which is of course the same chronological age.*

*Pictures **1a** and **b**, **2**, **3a** and **b** are the result of an ultrastructural study by A S Zelickson MD, J H Mottaz, J S Weiss MD, C N Ellis MD, and J H Vorhees MD, presented via the proceedings of Emerging Role of Retinoids in the treatment of Aging and Skin Cancer, March 11-13, 1988; Miami, Florida, USA, and published in the Journal of Cutaneous Aging and Cosmetic Dermatology; Volume 1, Number 1, 1988, page 14. Picture **4** was taken by Dr Peter Berger.*

is a direct relationship between one's outlook on life and ageing. Anger, fear, frustration and other stresses appear to weaken the immune system and speed the ageing process. On the other hand, a positive, healthy outlook on life gives one peace of mind and slows the ageing process. So beauty really does come from within. A relaxed, fit person generally has a smile and a serenity which inevitably makes them look and feel young.

The key to managing stress is first to recognise it. Perhaps you feel depressed, anxious, or have low self-esteem. Or perhaps you feel angry, frustrated, irritable and constantly exhausted. You may even feel shortness of breath, chest tightness, and difficulty getting to sleep, or develop skin rashes. In order to cope adequately with stress you must first identify the cause and seek out the appropriate skill to help you handle it better. Some of these methods are discussed more fully in the next chapter.

REVERSING AGEING SKIN CHANGES

There are several other options available for reversing some of the ageing skin changes. These range from quite simple office procedures to more complicated rejuvenating surgery. They include the following, which will be discussed in detail:

1. Chemosurgery
2. Dermabrasion
3. Collagen implants
4. Removal of growths
5. Plastic surgery.

1. CHEMOSURGERY
This procedure involves the application of certain caustic chemicals to the skin, causing peeling. The two most frequently used chemicals are trichloracetic acid (TCA) in varying strengths, or phenol. Which chemical, and what strength used, depends on the site treated and the purpose intended. The chemicals remove the epidermis and sometimes the upper part of the dermis,

67

depending on what result is required. Essentially, chemosurgery is a controlled second-degree chemical burn. After the peel the treated skin gradually sloughs off and fresh new skin regenerates.

Chemosurgery is used to either peel the whole face or just to treat limited areas. Full-face peels, using either 50 per cent TCA or phenol, are very effective in removing most of the changes associated with photo-ageing. The possibility of side effects, however, is much greater using phenol. TCA is much safer to use, and may result in significant skin improvement, but may need to be repeated from time to time. Limited area peels are useful in removing solar lentigines and other areas of uneven, blotchy pigmentation on the face or hands. Fine wrinkles around the eyes and mouth respond particularly well. The vertical lines over the upper lip, that cause lipstick to 'bleed', can also be smoothed. Superficial chemical peeling is also sometimes used before the regular use of tretinoin cream to speed up the rejuvenating changes.

Not everyone is suited to chemosurgery. In general, fair-complexioned people respond better than do those with dark complexions. This is largely because the colour contrast after treatment is less, and the chance of uneven pigmentation as a complication of treatment is also less.

The treatment is carried out as an office procedure. Sometimes mild sedation and analgesia may be used. The desired result determines the appropriate chemical and dilution selected. Within seconds of the application of the chemical, a burning sensation is felt, and within minutes the skin goes white. After half to one hour the area is red and swollen, and pain free after twenty-four hours. Over the next ten days the darkened, dry skin peels off. Make-up can usually be used to cover up after twenty-four to forty-eight hours. The new, rejuvenated skin that forms must be well protected from sunlight for the next two to three months.

Chemosurgery is not a panacea for all the degenerative changes associated with skin ageing. There are possible complications, and not everyone is suited to the procedure. If it is something you wish to consider, it is important to select a dermatologist experienced in its use.

2. DERMABRASION

This is a surgical technique involving planing of the skin using an abrasive tool. It results in the removal of the damaged epidermis and upper dermis, allowing regeneration of undamaged skin from below. This procedure has been used for many years for the removal of deeper wrinkles and scars. It cannot, of course, remove all wrinkles or scars, but it can make them much less obvious.

Dermabrasion can be performed without general anaesthesia, as an office procedure. Hospitalisation is not necessary. The facial skin is anaesthetised by freezing with a skin refrigerant. This also stiffens the skin so there is a firm basis for abrading. Then a very rapidly rotating wire brush or diamond fraise is stroked across the skin to plane or smooth it, much as wood is planed or sanded smooth. Swelling, and then extensive crusting, will appear in the first forty-eight hours. These crusts will gradually come off during the next ten to fifteen days, leaving the new underlying skin thinner, smoother and pinker than before. It will also be more sun sensitive, and needs maximal protection for the following three to four months. After two weeks, make-up may be worn, and full recovery usually takes about six weeks. Again, fair-skinned people are more suited to this procedure. Complications, such as scarring and pigmentation changes, can occur. The procedure is often done in conjunction with a facelift for wrinkling, but on its own mainly for acne scarring.

3. COLLAGEN IMPLANTS

Collagen is a natural protein that provides structural support. It is found throughout the body—in skin, muscle, tendon and bone. Collagen is basically a long-chain protein formed of three fibrils twisted around one another, forming a rope-like triple helix. These fibres are then woven together like threads in fabric to form a supportive framework providing texture, resilience and shape to the skin. Human collagen is very similar to the collagen found in certain animals. Consequently, animal collagen has many medical applications. For example, it is used for sutures and heart valves. Injectable collagen is made from cow skin that has been highly purified. Being so similar to human collagen, it is accepted by the body and becomes an integral part of the recipient's skin.

Currently two types of collagen are available: the un-cross-linked (Zyderm), which means the fibres are separate from each other and when injected become linked; and the partially cross-linked (Zyplast). The former is able to be re-absorbed by the body more quickly than the latter. Both lend additional support to weakened areas in the collagen network—otherwise known as wrinkles! The material is injected directly under the wrinkle, or depressed scar, which then raises it to the level of the surrounding skin. Thus the line, or scar, is minimised.

Collagen implants are particularly useful in correcting 'smoker's wrinkles'—those vertical lines around the mouth; 'drooler's crease'—the lines running downward from the corners of the mouth; and 'frown lines'—the vertical creases between the eyebrows. Some actresses are also now using collagen to increase the size of their lips and to accentuate their 'pout'. However, the effect on the lips is short lived.

1. Collagen exists to provide structural support.

2. Here, animal collagen has been injected directly under the depressed area, or wrinkle, to add texture and make the skin surface more even.

1. Collagen injections can rebuild the creases between the eyebrows.

2. *Collagen implants can correct vertical lines around the mouth.*

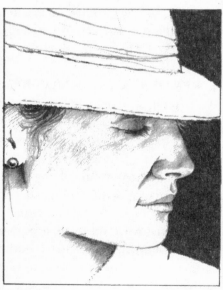

4. Collagen will strengthen furrows between the nose and mouth.

3. *Collagen can fillout the lines running from the corners of the mouth.*

Collagen implants are not suitable for everyone. Some people (about 2 per cent) are allergic to it. Therefore, everyone must have a small test dose in the arm, one month prior to intended treatment, to ensure they are not allergic. Also, anyone with a history of autoimmune disease or an allergy to local anaesthetics is unable to have this treatment. The procedure is quick and painless because the needles used are extremely thin and the collagen is also mixed with a little local anaesthetic. Slight swelling and bruising is evident immediately afterwards, but settles within less than twelve hours.

Like most good things in life, the effect achieved does not last forever. The implant will be altered like one's own collagen by the same ongoing mechanical forces, such as frowning, and the same biochemical processes of ageing. Most implants, though, last between six and twelve months before a 'top up' may be necessary. With each top up, less collagen is usually required. It is not necessary to always have further implants because if you choose not to, the skin correction will subside gradually until your skin looks as it did before treatment.

4. REMOVAL OF COMMON BENIGN GROWTHS

With both genetic and photo-ageing, harmless skin growths eventually begin to sprout. There are a number of simple, quick and inexpensive office procedures available to deal with these. It is worthwhile being aware that these exist, and you should not be frightened to enquire about whether they would be suitable for getting rid of spots and lumps that you dislike. Many patients have put up with lesions that were unsightly because of the fear that, if interfered with, they might become malignant; or thought that they were burdens meant to be endured; or that their removal might mean expensive surgery; or even that the doctor may dismiss their desires as frivolous vanity.

Cryotherapy

This is the use of freezing to destroy unwanted tissue. Freezing causes the death of cells, mainly by the formation of ice in the tissues outside the cell. The cell is then destroyed by the water being drawn from it, causing an overconcentration of chemicals within the cell.

Liquid nitrogen is the most commonly used freezing agent, either applied with a cotton bud or sprayed on. It freezes the tissue to a temperature of –197°C. One treatment is usually sufficient, and the amount of time the liquid nitrogen is in contact with the tissues depends on the type of growth, its size and its depth. The treatment is not usually painful, although it is accompanied by a stinging or burning sensation which peaks with thawing, two minutes after treatment. Within six to twelve hours a blister may form. This dries in two to three days, leaving a scale which takes about two weeks to fall off. Cryosurgery poses virtually no risk of scarring, although there may be some loss of pigmentation.

Lesions most suited to this form of treatment include:

Seborrhoeic keratoses: These are very common growths of middle to late life. They are a yellowish-brown, raised and scaly, greasy and crumbly, and may enlarge and blacken. They are not warts and are quite harmless, albeit unsightly, with a strong familial tendency.

Solar keratoses ('sun spots'): These are dry and rough, usually quite small, and may appear red. Often they are tender to touch and irritated by sunlight. Solar keratoses are not the same as skin cancers.

Solar lentigines ('age or liver spots'): These only appear on sun-damaged or photo-aged skin. They vary in size from a half to five centimetres in diameter, and in colour from light to very dark brown. They are not the same as freckles.

Electrosurgery

This technique uses a high-frequency, alternating electric current, to actually dehydrate unwanted growths. Heat is applied to the tissue using a fine probe through which the current passes. The growth is destroyed by small bursts of sparks which coagulate the tissue. The procedure is painless because it is usually performed under local anaesthesia or with only a very small current.

The lesions most usually treated in this manner include:

Milia (small sebaceous cysts): These closely resemble whiteheads and many can be removed quickly and painlessly by electrosurgery.

Acrochordons ('skin tags'): These are small flesh-coloured, benign growths that usually hang on fine stalks. They are most frequently found on the sides of the neck, eyelids and armpits. Skin tags may also be light brown in colour, and tend to have a familial tendency also.

Telangiectasia ('broken capillaries'): These are small dilated blood vessels that appear on the face of photo-aged individuals or those suffering with rosacea. They are more common in women, due, it is thought, to oestrogen exposure over the years. Here, a very fine probe is placed into the vessel, which is sealed by the heat produced from the small electric current.

Solar lentigines: Some doctors prefer this method to cryotherapy because it is more accurate and less likely to leave post-treatment pigmentation.

Seborrhoeic keratoses: Those too thick to treat with cryotherapy are best treated by electrosurgery.

Curettage

This is a kind of surgical skin-scraping performed with a special instrument, called a curette. It is a cutting instrument with an oval, loop-shaped cutting edge and handle. These are available in various sizes. For small lesions they may be used without local anaesthesia. However, most commonly a curette is used with local anaesthesia and in conjunction with electrosurgery.

Lesions treated by this method include:

Sebaceous adenomata (overgrown oil glands): These are usually round, lobulated and yellowish or waxy-looking lumps. They are normally multiple, and on the face of middle-aged to elderly males predominantly.

Seborrhoeic keratoses.

Milia.

Shave excision

This is an excellent method for removing growths elevated above the skin surface. Following the administration of local anaesthesia, a scalpel is used in a horizontal, back and forth motion, thereby shaving the unwanted growth from the surrounding skin. The wound beneath heals by itself without requiring sutures. Because it is very superficial there is generally little risk of scarring. This method also enables a specimen of the tissue to be sent to pathology for analysis if required. It is an excellent way to remove large raised skin lesions, in particular moles.

Moles

Mole, 'beauty spot', or birthmark are all terms for the same thing—a *naevus*. This is simply a benign overgrowth of pigment cells. Moles may be flesh-coloured or vary from light to dark brown. They may be flat or raised, have broad bases, or grow on stalks, and can range in size from a pinhead to several centimetres. They should never be removed by destructive means such as electro or chemosurgery, because adequate pathology analysis is then not possible. The advantage of shave excision is that the mole can be 'sculpted' away from the underlying and surrounding skin whilst preserving the general contours of the region, leaving a minimal, slightly paler area where the mole had been. However, because part of the mole below the surface remains, regrowth, or darkening, of the treatment site occasionally occurs later. This is infrequent, though, and the area can easily be touched up with light electrosurgery in a matter of minutes.

Excision and suture

Here the skin lesion is cut out under local anaesthesia in the shape of an ellipse. The length of the cut will usually be at least two-thirds longer than the lesion itself. This is necessary to enable the resulting wound to be brought together in a line without distortion. The wound is then drawn together into a fine line by stitches, which are removed after three to seven days, depending on the site.

No matter what method of removal is used, some scarring must be expected. Whenever the continuity of the skin is breached, some mark to indicate this will be visible. The methods discussed usually leave only minimal marks, but it is impossible to leave none. Unfortunately, some individuals heal less well than others, and this cannot be foreseen or prevented. To achieve the best cosmetic result, the direction of the cut is carefully chosen to blend with the natural tension and wrinkle lines of the skin. To prevent cross-hatching from stitches, ultra-fine material is used, and removed as soon as practical. New dressings, which keep the area moist whilst healing occurs and which minimise infection, are frequently used as well.

Laser

The word LASER stands for Light Amplification by Stimulated Emission of Radiation. Simply stated, lasers are very intense, highly focused, powerful beams of light. Different lasers produce lights of different wavelengths, which have different properties and therefore different applications. Various machines are now being used, including the Argon Laser, the Carbon Dioxide Laser, the Copper Vapour Laser and the Tunable Dye Laser. No doubt others will appear.

Basically, the laser produces yellow and green lights that are specifically absorbed by dark pigments such as haemoglobin (which gives blood its red colour), melanin (a natural tanning pigment) and dyes (used in tattoos). The laser beam penetrates the epidermis and targets the red colour in the capillaries, and is absorbed by the red-coloured haemoglobin in blood. This results in the production of intense heat, which destroys the capillaries. The laser light is shone on and traced along each superficial blood vessel. It feels like a pin scratching the surface of the skin. The skin may redden and occasionally blister after treatment. A scab then forms, and healing takes one to two weeks. Treatment, if necessary, may be repeated after two to three months, and scarring, if it occurs, is minimal.

The following lesions are amenable to laser treatment.

Superficial blood vessel problems: These include widespread telangiectasia ('broken capillaries') of the face, port-wine birthmarks and severe rosacea of the nose. Superficial leg veins are not suited to laser treatment because they are too deep and large. If treated, scarring may result and the veins are likely to return.

Pigment cell malformations: These include some birthmarks, multiple freckles and solar lentigines. Sometimes skin tags and very resistant warts may also respond.

Tattoos: These may respond well if they are small.

Laser treatment is not a space-age cure-all, and is not without its risks. Scarring and pigment loss are the commonest complications. These are unlikely to occur if appropriate lesions are treated with the appropriate type of laser. Unfortunately, some laser operators, having bought expensive machinery, are tempted to use it no matter what! Laser treatment is expensive, and the applications are very limited. It is wise to check whether the lesion you want treated may not be better managed with some other more suitable, and possibly less expensive, means.

Sclerotherapy

This is the technique of injecting inside superficial, dilated veins, causing them to be obliterated. The injected solution irritates the wall of the vein, damaging it. A tiny thrombus, or clot, then forms, and the blood flow stops. The vein is then turned into a 'cord' of blood and fibrous tissue that slowly is re-absorbed by the body, leaving an area of normal-looking skin.

Various solutions, or sclerosants, may be used—the three commonest being Dextrose (a sugar solution), Hypertonic Saline (a strong salt solution) and a chemical, Sodium Tetradecyl Sulphate (STD).

So-called 'starbursts', dark red-blue on the legs mainly of females, are most suited to this treatment. Using a very fine needle, the solution is injected into the lumen of these superficial veins. This stings for a few minutes only. Afterwards, the leg is generally bandaged for one week. Occasionally, small clots may form, or pigment staining occur. These usually disappear in time. The results of this treatment are good, but of course not every single unsightly vein can be treated, and sometimes treated ones may recur.

5. PLASTIC SURGERY

If you put your fingers on the skin of your temple you will see how much you can move it, and how the skin around your eye is distorted when you do this. This is due to the skin's plasticity, or movability. A plastic surgeon is basically one skilled in the movement of skin and other tissues like fat, muscle, tendons, blood vessels and nerves. Some people imagine that they use plastic instead of sutures, and therefore perform 'scarless' surgery. Being skilled in the movement of skin, plastic surgeons can do what you could not with your temple skin—move it without distorting another part of the skin. They are skilled in many incredibly complex manoeuvres to move and reorientate skin and so redrape it over the facial bones and other structures. Furthermore, although 'scarless' surgery is impossible, they are able, with sophisticated techniques, to minimise and camouflage scars. They hide them inside hairlines, skin folds and wrinkles, so that they are virtually invisible.

Many of the procedures I have discussed for the rejuvenation of ageing skin may be performed by plastic surgeons as well as dermatologists. Generally, however, plastic surgery is performed under general anaesthesia, and frequently in hospital or day surgery centres.

Cosmetic plastic surgery mainly involves the face, because it is the most exposed and most visually obvious part of the body. It reflects our age, race, character, emotion, health and, of course, beauty. The treatment of an aged face includes treatment of the skin itself—which we have discussed—and the redraping of loose, sagging skin which involves the underlying supportive tissues as well. The latter requires quite major surgery. For this type of cosmetic facial surgery, the face is usually divided into three main areas:

1. The upper face—from the eyes up
2. The mid face—from the eyes down to the mouth
3. The lower face—from the mouth into the neck area.

1. Upper-face surgery

Ageing here causes brow ptosis. This gives one a tired or angry look. Following a coronal lift, forehead lift or direct brow lift, one has a happier, more alert look. The choice of surgery depends on the hairline, the width of the forehead and the sex of the patient.

2. Mid-face surgery

Ageing here causes loose skin to fall forwards and downwards towards the nose, increasing the lines between the nose and the lips with excessive skin and fat deposits in the upper and lower eyelids. To correct this a mid-face lift, or temporo-periorbital-malarplasty may be performed. This is usually done in conjunction with a blepharoplasty, or removal of the excess eyelid skin and fat.

3. Lower-face surgery

Ageing here mostly takes the form of jowl lines, double chin and 'turkey neck'. This can be corrected with dramatic effects by a lower-face and upper-neck lift. This also involves tightening of the underlying supportive tissue, and often liposuction of excessive fat.

Other areas of the body age also, but not as rapidly as the face, because they are not normally exposed to UV light for 365 days a year. Surgical improvement to the breasts, stomach, buttocks and legs are all possible these days. It is important, however, to remember that there are always risks associated with such surgery, and that these operations are by no stretch of the imagination minor ones. Neither are the operations without scars. Finally, it is important to ensure that you are referred to an approved and skilled surgeon and, if necessary, do not be embarrassed to ask for a second opinion before proceeding with surgery.

6

Improve your skin

For this is the great error of our day . . . That physicians separate the soul from the body.

Plato

PSYCHE AND THE SKIN

There is a very close relationship between what goes on in the mind and the state of the skin. There are a number of possible reasons for this, the first being that in the embryo stage, the skin is formed from the same substance as the brain—the ectoderm. The skin and the brain are probably the most fascinating and complicated organs of the body. Like the brain, the skin is still to be fully explored and understood.

Second, the bond between the skin and the mind may well be related to there being more nerve pathways leading to the brain from the skin than from any other organ. These can relay messages to and from the brain faster than the speed of light, instantly recording pleasure, pain, touch, temperature or irritation. It is estimated that in just one square centimetre of skin you will find approximately one hundred sweat glands, ten hairs, one metre of blood vessels, four metres of nerve fibres, hundreds of nerve endings programmed to record pain, twenty-five pressure receptors sensitive to tactile stimuli, two sensory receptors to record cold, twelve sensory receptors to record heat, countless lymph vessels, and fifteen sebaceous glands.

The skin also acts as an important erogenous zone. It is now well understood how important for infants is the effect of stroking, and caressing, for satisfactory emotional development. Similarly, the skin has important sexual connotations, as well as being of great psychological importance to us with respect to our external appearance.

Nothing ever happens in our minds that does not affect our bodies, and the reverse is also true. The skin is paramount among all the body organs as an instrument of expression. Everyone knows that blushing signifies embarrassment, that anger provokes flushing, that fear is expressed in blanching, that sweating is a response to excessive emotional excitement. Presumably such reactions were, in ancient times, appropriate to some emergency, preparing our ancestors for some form of useful defence. In modern society these reactions have lost their functional aspect because of social disapproval of the expression of primitive instinctual drives; for us blushing, pallor and sweating are cutaneous signs by which the inhibited instincts are betrayed. The manifestations of emotions in the skin are brought about chiefly by neural discharges within the autonomic nervous system and changes in hormones from the endocrine system. There is a very close association between both these systems and the skin.

Obviously, then, the mind will most definitely influence the type and timing of various skin disorders, and conversely, these disorders will affect the mind. Some doctors deny that the psyche has any other than a superficial relationship to skin disorders, insisting upon organic causes in every case. Others may see the psyche lurking behind every pimple. It is a clinical fact that patients often react more strongly emotionally to skin diseases that are freely visible than to far more serious internal, and consequently hidden, disorders. The skin occupies a special place in the human psyche, being a kind of outermost representative of the ego. The slightest blemish may call forth deep hidden fears. A small patch of alopecia (hair loss) is not in itself a very serious symptom, but if the patient privately believes that it signifies loss of virility, his anxiety over the symptom may not seem so disproportionate. This then poses a special problem for the person making diagnoses. It is often quite difficult to know whether anxiety is causative or reactive; that is, whether the emotional distress caused the skin disease or the skin disease caused the anxiety. Often, of course, both factors are present in a vicious cycle. It may be true that skin diseases are not, on the whole, fatal, but it is also true that many of these disorders ruin a patient's emotional life.

STRESS AND MODERN LIVING

Most of us, at some time or other, feel 'stressed'. This may mean a number of things—being too busy, not having enough time in the day, worrying a lot and not knowing why, not sleeping well, feeling tense and irritable, or just generally depressed. Stress is really the body's reaction to stimulus and change.

These reactions include tensing of muscles, deep and fast breathing, increased heart rate, excessive perspiration, raised blood pressure and the release of adrenalin into the blood. This is to enable the person to deal with the situation that has caused the stress. Thousands of years ago, when humans hunted animals to eat and survival of the fittest was essential, this reaction of 'fight or flight' was appropriate. However, the situations which trigger these reactions now are quite different, and possibly the reaction has become inappropriate.

Some stresses are good, or pleasant. Some occur when you are enjoying yourself, such as playing sport, being promoted, playing music, or having sex. Although causing the same physical stress, these reactions are often described as excitement, stimulation, enjoyment or ecstasy. Without these pleasant stresses, life would be boring and unsatisfying—no doubt causing further stress!

Other stresses are bad, or unpleasant. The main ones are:

- Major lifestyle changes—getting divorced, retiring, unemployment.
- Unexpected events—death of a loved one, sudden loss of job, illness.
- Accumulated events—work stress, marital problems, study.

Minor stresses may include traffic jams, having nowhere to park the car, sitting exams, moving house, and even marriage.

Everyone reacts differently to the same situation. What is stressful to one person may be ordinary to another, enjoyable to a third person and unpleasant to a fourth. So what causes one person to be stressed may not affect another. Also, what may stress you this year may not the following, because either you have adapted to it or learned to cope with it. It all depends on your personality, or mental make-up. Stress only becomes a problem if there is too much of it, if it is too prolonged, or if you are unable to deal with it. Emotional problems, behaviour problems or stress-induced illness may result.

All of us are at risk of having a stress-related problem because we all let things get on top of us from time to time. Some of us, of course, are more at risk than others. Those who worry a lot, are overly ambitious, exacting or even perfectionist, impatient, demanding of self and others, and intensely competitive, are also inevitably very stressed. These people have a strong need for recognition and success, and often over-reach themselves by setting goals that everyone else knows are unattainable. Their inner instability is often masked by outward calm, and although they tend to be overachievers, they suffer from feelings of inadequacy that only drive them to push themselves even harder. They constantly operate under a heavy load of anxiety and fear of failure that results in a very high level of self-generated tension.

Unfortunately, living in a modern society presents daily stresses that can make too many demands on us physically, mentally and emotionally. We are simply not adapting to these stresses satisfactorily. If, in the middle of the night, somebody makes a loud noise outside, we are instantly awake, with our hearts pounding, breathing deeply—keyed up for action. This is a normal reaction to the stimulus. However, people today go around permanently keyed up in much the same way. This chronic stress, if it continues, causes the body to adapt to it. From the outside, all looks well. Our body has adapted to the stress. However, in order to do this, every defence available has been mustered, and of course this can only last for a short time before the body burns itself out. A 'burnout' will happen when all this adaptation fails and some organ 'collapses'. This may take the form of a psychological illness, a peptic ulcer, asthma, hypertension, or a skin disorder such as one of the following.

Itchiness: A severe or even mild itch, whether local or generalised, is, in the absence of any prior external or internal disease, most likely to be psychogenic. Often this itch may occur in an area highly endowed with nerve endings, such as around the genitals or the anal area. Various possible psychological reasons and explanations have been given for this particular symptom. These include displaced sexual gratification; a need for self-inflicted injury to satisfy masochistic impulses; the relief of tension by the neuro-muscular exercise of scratching; and the expression of shame, guilt or exhibitionistic traits.

Eczema: There are forms of eczema, all occurring in adults, that are thought to have a strong emotional basis. These are: the so-called discoid eczema, which occurs in coin-shaped spots, mainly on the limbs, and which is extremely itchy; dyshidrotic eczema, which occurs about the fingers and toes as small, itchy bubbles under the skin; and lichen simplex, which is a well-localised thickened area of skin that is extremely itchy. Lichen simplex may occur on any area of the body, but always in an easily accessible place. Sufferers of these forms of eczema obviously require treatment to the skin and, in addition, an understanding doctor to help them sort out, or at least talk over, their underlying problems or anxieties.

Trichotillomania: This is not such a rare condition, but it is one that frequently goes unrecognised in its minor form. Principally, it occurs in children who seek neurotic satisfaction through pulling out their own hair. Usually they select the hair of the scalp, and less often the eyebrows. The principal element in the psychodynamic of these children is the turning on oneself of unexpressed rage at rejecting parents. This is the transformation of a sadistic instinct into a masochistic one.

Hair pulling may be missed as the cause of hair loss if it is not considered in relation to patients thought to have ringworm, alopecia areata, etc.

Adults who inflict this condition on themselves are often deeply disturbed individuals, usually with sexual conflicts that, basically, revolve around the notion that sex is dirty, and repugnant; they contrive to 'shed' these feelings by pulling out their hair and making themselves less likely objects of sexual attention.

Parasitophobia: This relates to a morbid fear of being infested with parasites. Sufferers of this condition may also be deluded, believing themselves already infested, and may bring in various pieces of thread, lint, scrapings and debris of all sorts believing them to be the 'parasites'. The deluded victims often have hallucinations, insisting that they can see and feel the parasites within their skin. Patients with this disorder require psychiatric help, as they frequently 'need' the symptom to remain, in other areas of their functioning life, sane.

Dermatitis artefacta: This is a skin disorder that is self-inflicted. Furthermore, the patient denies having produced the lesion with his or her own hands. Chemicals, heat, or other physical and mechanical means may be used to inflict the disorder, and the lesions are therefore of singularly curious patterning, generally not conforming to known disorders and usually in an easily accessible area. A fairly decisive diagnostic indication is the disappearance of the lesion under an occlusive dressing.

Generally speaking, two types of patient perpetrate this type of disorder: the hysterical individual, with a rather apathetic appearance, who converts intense anxiety into this symptom; and the malingering individual, who produces the lesion to attain some gain or to explain a lack of success. These patients require help, and should certainly not be confronted or accused of self-infliction. Psychiatric referral is wise.

We are all ridden with various anxieties and tensions of differing degree. It is therefore essential that we develop, or improve, our facilities for reducing these tensions or anxieties, so that we may live within the capabilities of our own particular skin. Those of us who have problems with the skin will, I am sure, have noticed how its condition is rather like a barometer, signifying very clearly how calm or distressed our internal milieu is.

Nevertheless, an individual with anxiety or tension symptoms may have a skin disorder that is unrelated to his or her stresses. Moreover, some disorders may occur more frequently in neurotic people yet not be caused by their neurosis, just as atopic eczema occurs in people with a tendency for allergies although eczema is rarely allergic. Likewise, the flaring up of a skin lesion following an emotional upset is not necessarily proof of psychogenic origin. Psychic factors often 'trigger' an eruption that can be easily misinterpreted as a psychogenic disease. For instance, an attack of herpes simplex may be precipitated by emotion, but it is not psychogenic—rather, the causative factor is a virus.

The reverse of this situation is the crediting of a therapeutic result to some physical therapy—such as creams, tablets, etc.— when in reality unrecognised psychological components in the therapy are responsible. When one doctor gets good results by dietary means, another by allergic management, another by eradicating foci of infection, and when the practitioner of one school is unable to repeat the results of the other, there is a strong likelihood that the factor common to all is psychological. Large doses of the doctor him or herself are often the curative agent.

On the surface the doctor–patient relationship is one in which a sick person requests help from an individual trained in medical science. There is, however, an emotional substratum, often not recognised by either party, having to do with one of the oldest relationships in human life: that between parent and child. Even in these sophisticated and perhaps sceptical days, the patient unconsciously fits the doctor into the prototype of the wise, omnipotent, loving, giving, parent, and much of the benefit of any type of treatment derives from this transference. It must, however, be remembered that many general physicians and specialists are extremely stress-ridden themselves—indicated by frequency of heart attacks, suicide etc.—and this may be one of the reasons many of their patients are turning to less conventional methods of stress relief.

STRESS AND HOW TO COPE

There are many ways of coping with stress. We all have the need, and the potential then, to change what may be damaging and destructive into what is creative and constructive. The first step in learning to cope is to *recognise the symptoms* of stress that you have. Second, you must *identify the cause* of the stress. Finally, you must *modify your reaction* to the stress.

There are many ways you can help yourself to handle stress better.

SUPERFICIAL PSYCHOTHERAPY

This is the most basic form of stress relief practised by both professional and non-professional alike. Here, the patient is encouraged to talk about his or her problems and anxieties to an individual who will be sympathetic and supportive. One does not have to be a psychiatrist to qualify as an audience, of course. Many people turn to a tolerant friend; and for centuries the clergy filled this role—many of them still do. However, the impersonality of professionals, their skilled prompting and therapeutic intent, give them a great advantage. A disadvantage is their costliness, but that reinforces the impersonality and also makes the process more purposeful for the patient. It gives the patient, to put it bluntly, a financial motive for recovery.

Sensitive physicians practise this form of supportive psychotherapy intuitively. Their patients are made to feel that they are worthwhile, and that the doctor wants more than anything in the world to help them. As a result of his or her warm, friendly, positive attitude, the physician enables the patient to feel secure, accepted, protected, less anxious and encouraged towards health. The aim is not to remake the patient's personality but to help an individual over a rough spot in his or her life. Advice may be given about rest, exercise, diet, use of drugs, hobbies etc., and sympathetic counselling about dealing with practical issues. With reassurance and support, the doctor reinforces the patient's defences against anxiety, emphasises his or her capacity to get well, and encourages self-esteem. This provides patients with a corrective emotional experience, with someone who treats them differently from everyone else in their life.

Frequently, counselling is necessary in order to satisfactorily modify your behaviour. You may need to overcome inner conflicts, to stop living with irrational assumptions about yourself, to find new and more appropriate forms of behaviour, or to learn to relate to people more satisfyingly. Professional advice, usually from a psychologist, may be very helpful in this area.

This type of therapy is, of course, quite different from the analytic type practised by psychiatrists. The latter is aimed at uncovering unconscious material and allowing it to be aired, in the hope that a permanent change in personality can be effected. Analysis, which is in the realm of psychiatric treatment may, in severe cases, be required.

It is interesing, however, to note that rashes of the type seen in neurodermatitis are a result of unresolved conflict. People with psychiatric diseases, however, have virtually given up the struggle to resolve their conflicts, and therefore the incidence of stress-related skin diseases amongst such individuals is very small.

RELAXATION EXERCISES

Relaxation is a skill that often needs to be learned. When you have mastered the technique, it can reduce your level of stress and minimise tension and anxiety. It allows you to do more, with less effort, and promotes a general feeling of wellbeing, with much less muscle tension. With regular practice your relaxation technique will allow you to let off energy that builds up in stressful situations.

One common method is to sit in a comfortable chair, or lie on your back with your head and knees supported by pillows. Tight clothing should be loosened. Breath slowly and regularly, saying the word 'relax' to yourself each time you breathe out. Think about different parts of your body, allowing each part to relax as you continue to breathe regularly and say the word 'relax'. Start with your toes and work upwards: calf muscles, thighs, abdomen, fingers, upper arms, small of the back, back of the neck and shoulders, and finally the little muscles around the eyes and brow.

Note any special areas of tension, and give them a little more time. The more often you relax, the more easily you can do it. Try to set aside a regular time once or twice each day for about ten to twenty minutes' relaxation.

BODY FITNESS

Health aside, being in good physical shape is, of course, simply very pleasant. Certainly it is extremely beneficial to the health of our cardiovascular system. In practice, though, physicians find it quite difficult to recommend exercise as treatment. The patient simply nods, eyeing the prescription pad. Why not a pill, he or she is thinking. The doctor explains that the patient will not be as tired, or as irritable, or as itchy, if he or she plays more tennis, takes long walks, jogs and so forth.

But as the patient gets dressed again, he or she may feel worse than ever. Exercise! How can I exercise when I am already too tired to get through the day? What such patients perhaps do not realise is that their chronic tiredness is a manifestation of their various anxieties and tensions, which are 'burning them up inside'.

It has been shown that an adequate exercise program improves not only physical fitness but also mental abilities. Carefully controlled trials have shown that speed of performance of intellectual tasks, memory and learning ability are all improved following a ten-week exercise program. Psychological testing following such a program has also shown that the person tested appears more content and less anxious. The mechanism by which exercise improves these factors is not known.

Exercise is most useful in another way too. It is a method of dispelling one of our most potent stresses, namely hostile aggression. This, unfortunately, is not only a collective national trait but a personal one too, lying deep within each one of us. It powers not only our careers, our games and our drama, but also the way we drive a car. The type of work most of us do involves less and less physical exertion. Hence, one of the many stresses we suffer from is the stress of our own pent-up aggressive drives. One way of dispelling these is by physical exercise.

YOGA

Yoga means union, a meeting; it is a state in which one unites, becomes one with, or attunes oneself to, reality. It is a union of your body and the physical aspects of your being with your mind, so that the body and mind can function harmoniously. Through yoga, some people can attain complete self-control.

The first step is to learn correct breathing; this has particular importance in yoga, and is thought to be essential for adequate control of the mind.

The next important step is a series of exercises known as Hatha Yoga. These exercises lead to correction of posture faults, and increased general fitness. Systematic relaxation is another very important aspect of yoga, and this also involves exercises, both to control and relax each part of the body.

Once these things have been mastered, the mind is ready for meditation. This may or may not be an essential part of anxiety reduction. There is no doubt, however, that yoga not only improves physical fitness, but also endows practitioners with an inner calm and an ability to cope with stresses that they were previously unable to manage.

ENCOUNTER GROUPS

These are also sometimes called sensitivity groups, and are not to be confused with more orthodox group therapy. Encounter groups are larger, up to say eighteen members, and sometimes have no official leader, whilst there is always a qualified therapist running the more orthodox groups. Encounter groups focus on 'personal difficulties', and often specialise in specific problem areas, such as stress in a corporate situation or in an unhappy marriage.

These groups commenced in the United States in the 1960s, and have been described as treatment for people who are not sick but simply seeking fulfilment. Nevertheless, their aims are decidedly therapeutic. They seek to make individuals feel human again, at ease with their own emotions and those of the people around them; they seek to counter the depersonalising effects of the industrial society in which many of us live. They constitute a kind of mass folk therapy, and it is estimated that some two million Americans have so far been moved to join them.

Within these groups, the veneer of politeness has to be lifted, masks must disappear. It is the opposite of the usual cocktail party situation. Physical routines may be used to get things started, such activities as closing one's eyes and groping, letting oneself fall backwards into another's arms, and hand wrestling. When doing psychodrama, the group members are told to act out experiences that have given them distress in the past—perhaps, a family quarrel. Then the group rotates roles, and so each member may move from acting out his problems to getting to see himself from other angles. There are limits to what encounter groups can accomplish and, very occasionally, there are dangers involved. Psychotic breakdowns under group pressure, though rare, have happened. The group member who returns alone into the everyday world can carry with him certain misconceptions of reality. He has changed, but the world has not. It is possible that Alcoholics Anonymous bears out what Dr Pratt discovered in Boston: that the greatest benefit from groups is gained by those people caught in the same specific stress problem, be it alcohol, skin disorders, or alienation.

MEDITATION

Another practice being used for stress relief, which is the polar opposite of encounter groups, is meditation. The most widespread and easily accessible technique is called Transcendental Meditation. It first caught the headlines in 1967, when the Beatles and Mia Farrow tripped off to the Himalayas to learn about it from the Maharishi Mahesh Yogi.

Individuals practising T.M. sit down and close their eyes for two periods of twenty minutes a day, during which time they, in effect, leave the stress battlefield, willing themselves into a state called 'restful alertness'. They do this by concentrating on the silent repetition of a word called a mantra, a soothing meaningless sound secretly assigned to each student by the instructor.

After commencing meditation, various things may occur. Frequently there is a marked increase in the number of dreams during sleep. This is thought to be very beneficial, since we all need to dream at night whether or not we remember our dreams the next morning. It has been demonstrated that people who do not dream enough become tense and anxious. Dreams, fantasies, trances and hallucinations are all forms of consciousness expansion and are enriching experiences. Physiologists have shown that in meditation there is a marked reduction of oxygen consumption; the reduction is greater than that of a person after six hours of sleep. Similarly, galvanic skin resistance, another positive key to relaxation, in some cases is increased fourfold.

In this and other movements derived from the East, diet is often involved, a vegetarian emphasis being common. Almost always there is also a degree of deliberate detachment from the turmoil of daily urban life, and a surrender to a group. This erasure of ego can produce a calm and may ease many life stresses.

BIOLOGICAL FEEDBACK

Behind bio-feedback lies something of a revolution in medical theory. Our muscles are obviously at the command of our will. We can force our arms to move up and down, our eyelids to blink fast or slowly. Until recently it had been thought that humans cannot consciously control their autonomic nervous system, the unseen regulator of such processes as pulse rate, glandular secretions, and oxygen consumption—the complex mechanisms that, when they go wrong, so frequently trigger the stress diseases.

Taking advantage of the many delicate electronic devices now available, doctors and psychologists have set up systems in which patients are kept continuously informed of what is going on within certain organs. For example, a blood pressure monitor may be set up in front of the subject. By concentrating on the monitor, the subject may learn to moderate his or her own blood pressure. Nobody knows how this is done, and the theories are many. The feedback is the vital element, the tool by which a patient learns control, and having learned it, the subject can sometimes then go back into the stressful world and control his or her visceral response without needing the visible feedback signal.

The brain itself emits different electrical signals during different activities. The highest-frequency signal, called beta, is emitted under pressure to complete tasks. Next down the scale is alpha, reflecting a more relaxed and contemplative mood. Then comes theta, associated with creative thinking; and delta, the lowest frequency, that comes with sleep. This brainwave activity can be monitored with special instruments. It has been demonstrated that people can be trained, through feedback, to shift their brains from beta to alpha, and sometimes even to theta waves. Here again, then, is a method that some people may use in certain circumstances to modify their anxiety levels.

HYPNOSIS

Hypnosis is essentially a state of mind, one that is usually induced in one person by another. It is attained by strict attention to either an object or to the repetitive spoken word. It results in a state of mind in which suggestions are not only more readily accepted than in the awake state, but are also acted upon much more powerfully than under normal conditions. Under hypnosis, one has access to the unconscious mind without the barrier of criticism normally presented by the conscious state. The actions and behaviour of a hypnotised subject may be compared with those of a person suffering from temporary absent-mindedness. Absent-mindedness is a state of mind that may come on suddenly and unexpectedly. It lasts for an indefinite period and then passes off equally suddenly. In such a state a person may start to do a job, and will do it just as efficiently and as thoroughly as in his normal state of mind. Yet when the absent-mindedness suddenly terminates, he or she will look and say: 'Good heavens, when did I start doing this?' The basic difference between the state of the hypnotised person and that of the absent-minded person is that under hypnosis a person's receptiveness to suggestion is tremendously enhanced. However, at no time is there loss of control. Your personality is always there, but may be likened to an 'observer'. Techniques for painless childbirth are essentially hypnosis techniques. Acupuncture is also a form of hypnosis, although other factors may also be involved.

Two specific aims of hypnotherapy are ego-strengthening and symptom removal. Under hypnosis it is relatively easy to instil in subjects a sequence of simple suggestions designed to remove tension, anxiety and apprehension, and to gradually restore the patients' confidence in themselves and in their ability to cope with their problems. Once this has been accomplished, one may successfully modify or remove specific symptoms, such as itching. Patients under hypnosis may also be guided, reassured, persuaded, and if necessary, reconditioned.

Depending on the nature of a patient's problem, he or she may then be taught the technique of self-hypnosis, and in certain circumstances, can be given a code word that, when recalled under appropriate circumstances, will facilitate the self-induction of a hypnotic, relaxed state. Some patients prefer to have a tape-recording made for them by the therapist, which they can use when circumstances demand it.

DRUGS

Unfortunately patients and many doctors have come to regard mood-altering drugs as a panacea for all kinds of social, physical and emotional ills. Interestingly enough, many people who would not think of taking alcohol do not seem to mind taking the various psychotrophic drugs available. Nevertheless, the most widely-used drug of all in our society is alcohol. It brings pleasure and relaxation when used carefully, yet misery and destruction when yielded to.

I believe that there is a place for placebos—pills that contain no medication but that nevertheless work because the patient believes they will work. In fact, many 'genuine' drugs are capable of curing people in part because of what is called a placebo effect. Bogus pills, or clinically inappropriate ones, are just the beginning of placebo medicine. Any treatment that has no definable curative powers but that nevertheless improves the patient's health, qualifies as such. This also applies to the miracles at Lourdes, and other examples of faith healing. The best placebo of all, in a way, may well be a good doctor-patient relationship.

It is, I believe, important to realise that the maxim 'A change is as good as a holiday' is not always true. Major events and changes in life—whether pleasant or unpleasant—invariably give rise to stress. Too much stress can, as seen, lead to physical illness. To avoid unnecessary ills, therefore, it is wise to order one's life in such a way as to ensure that changes do not occur too rapidly or drastically.

As it is the *amount* of change that matters—whether welcome or unwelcome—if possible, the individual should make preparations in advance to cope with the additional stress that major changes impose. If, for example, a person plans to retire, sell his house and move interstate, it would be wise for him to retire one year, and move interstate the next. This avoids the accumulation of too many changes in a short space of time.

It is also as well for doctors to be aware that patients quite rightly are going out after what they see as their own best cures, and sometimes leaving conventional medicine far behind them. It is easy for us to dismiss some of the techniques described in this chapter as esoteric entertainments of little practical value. This, however, would be an unfortunate conclusion, as many of the techniques described have helped many patients, particularly those with skin disorders. The physician should be able to understand and guide patients to the method of treatment most suited to their particular needs.

ITCHING

An itch is one of the commonest complaints relating to the skin. Frequently it is unaccompanied by any visible causative disease. Although everyone knows what an itch is, it is nevertheless difficult to define. The most widely accepted definition might be: 'that unpleasant sensation that provokes the desire to scratch'. Itching is an important symptom of many diseases of the skin, and also of internal disorders. It also warrants attention because of the further damage to the skin that would be caused by continued scratching.

Although itching has been extensively studied, its causes are ill understood. However, any discussion of itching must refer to the physiology, so that the limitations of treatment may be understood. Itching, then, is a disagreeable sensation produced by the action of stimuli of a harmful nature on the skin surface. It is a signal of actual or potential danger to the skin. The purpose of the reflex action of scratching is to remove the causative agent from the body surface.

It is thought that a wide variety of stimuli and noxious agents may liberate chemicals in the skin which then act on peripheral nerves, eliciting the itch sensation. These chemicals include histamine, bradykine, protease, and prostaglandins. Throughout the skin there are many itch receptors. On the forearm these points lie approximately one millimetre apart. However, they are more closely set in areas about orifices such as the mouth or anus. The small skin nerves carry the impulses to the spinal cord, from where they are transmitted via the pain fibres to the brain. It is not yet understood how scratching relieves itching, but possibly it disturbs the rhythm of the impulses travelling towards the spinal cord. Scratching may also simply damage the nerve fibres that are conveying the itch.

Inherent in the problem of itching is its subjective and elusive nature. Some people are 'itchers', others are not. Some itch intensely, others not at all. Allowing for this variation, the absence or presence of an itch, as well as its severity, may be of great diagnostic value. Of importance, also, might be the intensity and location of the itch, as well as the time of occurrence and the factors that provoke or relieve it.

As with pain, there are always two aspects of itching—how it is perceived and a person's reaction to it. Many psychological components influence the latter: anxiety, tension and fear, for instance, all of which will aggravate itching. In some individuals, itching is only relieved by the infliction of self-trauma, which replaces the itching with soreness, stinging or pain. In others, itching and rubbing is associated with pleasurable emotions, which have a sexual component; this reaction is termed *orgasme cutané*.

It must be remembered that an itch is a symptom, not a disease, and that there are a multitude of causes of itching. However, the vast majority of individuals who itch without visible evidence of skin disease, do so for some psychological reason.

POSSIBLE CAUSES OF ITCHING
1. Physical and chemical
• spicules, e.g. fibre glass, wool, detergent
• proteases, e.g. nettles, Rhus tree
• drugs, e.g. opiates, quinidine
2. Skin diseases
• obvious, e.g. eczema, tinea, bites
• not obvious, e.g. scabies, hives, winter itch
3. Internal diseases or conditions
• metabolic disorders, e.g. diabetes, thyroid disorders
• liver disorders
• kidney disorders
• blood disorders
• pregnancy
• cancer
• parasitic infestation
• iron deficiency
4. Psychological disorders
• parasitophobia
• depression

TREATMENT
The treatment of an itch will take two general forms. First, it is essential to treat the cause, whether it is curable or only controllable. Second, the itch itself should be relieved so that further skin damage does not occur, and the individual may remain sane.

Specific measures of treatment include adequate explanation of what is wrong and what is proposed to be done, so that the patient is involved with, and understands the aim of, the treatment.

Physical restraints, particularly with children, are most helpful as a means of preventing scratching and further skin damage. This may involve, for example, splinting of the arms; thick wrapping of the worst-affected areas; or the wearing of boxing gloves to bed.

Cooling of the worst-affected areas or of the whole body has a fairly specific anti-itch effect. This may be achieved by cold compresses, tar baths, and the avoidance of hot showers, electric blankets and excessive clothing. Simple applications such as calamine lotion, with menthol or phenol, also give relief due to their chilling action. The avoidance of hot drinks and alcohol can be most helpful.

Various common proprietary preparations may have a non-specific soothing action on an itch. These include calamine lotion, zinc cream, tar creams and anti-histamine creams. The latter should be completely avoided, as should local anaesthetic creams, because of their strong capacity to sensitise the skin and cause a contact dermatitis. Similarly, provocative influences such as friction from rough clothing should be avoided.

Topical corticosteroids (cortisone creams or ointments): These are very effective in diminishing the itch associated with certain conditions. This is probably due to their non-specific anti-inflammatory action. Some conditions, however, such as hives or drug allergies, are unresponsive. On the other hand, if they are used for treating an itch-condition that is itself responsive to corticosteroids, then both the primary disorder and the associated itch will settle. On rare occasions oral corticosteroids may be required, not for the itch itself, but to suppress the underlying disorder causing an itch.

Anti-histamines: Histamine is one of the best-known chemical causes of itching. Anti-histamines do not actually oppose the action of histamine, but act by blocking the receptor sites on the cells, to the exclusion of histamine. There are two such receptor sites, known as H_1 and H_2. The majority of anti-histamines only block the H_1 sites, whereas doxepin or the tricyclic anti-depressants and the anti-peptic-ulcer drug cimetidine, block the H_2 sites. Unfortunately they may also have a sedative effect, which is enhanced by alcohol. There are currently more than twenty anti-histamines available, and there is unfortunately very little evidence from which to make a rational choice between them. They do, however, fall into several different structural or chemical groups. This is useful to know, as individuals will vary in the way they

RELATIVE POTENCIES OF
TOPICAL CORTICOSTEROID PREPARATIONS

PRODUCT	FORMS	TRADE NAME	POTENCY
Betamethasone dipropionate 0.05% in propylene glycol	Cream, ointment	Diprosone O.V.	Highest potency
Clobetasol proplonate 0.05%	Cream, ointment, scalp lotion	Dermovate (UK)	
Diflucortolone valerate 0.3%	Oily cream, ointment	Nerisone Forte (UK)	
Halobetasol Propionate 0.05%	Cream, ointment	Ultravate (USA)	
Betamethasone dipropionate 0.05%	Cream, ointment, scalp lotion	Diprosone	Very potent
Betamethasone valerate 0.1%	Cream lotion, ointment, scalp application	Betnovate, Celestone V	
Clobetasone Botyrate 0.05%	Cream, oily cream	Eumovate (UK)	
Desonide 0.05%	Cream	Tridesilon (UK)	
Desoxymethasone 0.25%	Oily cream	Stiedex (UK)	
Diflorasone diacetate 0.05%	Cream, ointment	Florone (USA)	
Diflucortalone valerate 0.1%	Cream, oily cream, ointment	Nerisone	
Fluclorolone acetonide 0.025%	Cream, ointment	Topilar	
Fluocinonide 0.05%	Cream, ointment, solution, gel	Metosyn (UK)	
Fluprednidene acetate 0.1%		Decoderm	
Fluocortolone Pivalate 0.25% with Fluocinolone Acetonide 0.025%	Cream, ointment, solution	Synalar	
	Ointment		
Fluocortolone 0.25% with Fluocortolone Mexanoate 0.25%	Cream, ointment	Ultralan	
Flurandrenolone 0.0125%	Cream, ointment	Haelan	
Halcinonide 0.025% to 0.1%	Cream, ointment, solution	Halciderm	
Triamcinolone acetonide 0.05%	Cream, ointment	Kenalone	
Triamcinolone acetonide 0.1% with neomycin gramicidin, nystatin	Cream, ointment	Kenacomb	
Betamethasone valerate 0.05%	Cream, ointment	Betnovate 1/2, Celestone V 1/2	Moderately potent
Flumethasone pivalate 0.02%	Cream, ointment	Locacorten	
Fluocortolone pivalate 0.1% with fluocortolone hexanoate 0.1%	Cream, ointment, fatty ointment	Ultralan-D	
	Cream, ointment		
Fluocinolone acetonide 0.01%	Cream, ointment	Synlar 01	
Fluocortin butylester 0.75%	Cream, ointment	Vaspid (USA)	
Flurandrenolone 0.05%	Cream, ointment, lotion	Haelan X (UK)	
Triamcinolone Acetonide 0.02%	Cream, ointment	Aristocort	Mildly potent
Aclomethasone dipropionate 0.05%	Cream, ointment	Logoderm	
Hydrocortisone 1.0%	Cream	Egocort	
Hydrocortisone 0.5%	Cream	Dermaid	
Hydrocortisone 0.1%	Cream	Egocort 1/10	
Hydrocortisone Acetate 1.0%	Cream, ointment	Cortef, Dermacort, Hydrosone, Sigmacort, Squibb-HC	
Hydrocortisone Acetate 0.5%	Cream, ointment	Cortaid, Cortic	

respond to various anti-histamines. If one particular drug does not
suit, another should be selected, but from a different group:

Alkylamines
Chlorpheniramine (Piriton)
Brompheniramine (Dimetane)
Dexchlorpheniramine
(Avil, Polaramine)
Phenothiazines
Promethazine (Phenergan)
Trimeprazine (Vallergan)
Methdilazine (Dilosyn)
Ethylenediamines
Mepyramine (Anthisan)
Ethanolamines
Diphenhydramine (Benadryl)

Piperazines
Chlorcyclizine (Ancolan)
Piperdines
Cyproheptadine (Periactin)
(Antegan)
Diphenylpyraline (Histryl)
Others
Hydroxyzine (Atarax)
Azatadine (Zadine)
Mebhydrolin (Fabahistin)
Astemizole (Hismanal)
Terfenadine (Teldane)

Sedatives (tranquillisers) and anti-depressants: Inflammation of the
skin is similar to that occurring elsewhere in the body. Yet the
very nature of the skin imposes particular difficulties for treatment
which are not present to the same extent in other areas of medicine.
In particular, these difficulties involve the obvious visual impact
of skin problems; the very accessibility of the skin itself; the special
irritating quality of itching; the intense satisfaction associated with
scratching; and the overall psychological importance of skin.

A little reading of folklore and mythology soon indicates that
the skin has always had a particular place in our emotional life.
Everyday expressions such as 'he gets under my skin', or 'I am
getting hot under the collar', testify to this. Hair has a special
symbolic significance, hence it is often referred to as a person's
'crowning glory'. The long association of two dreaded diseases—
leprosy and syphilis—with the skin has also never been quite
forgotten.

Consequently, individuals with persistent and itchy skin diseases
easily become anxious and depressed, and the relief of these
symptoms must often play quite a major part in therapy.

Sedatives have a long history of being helpful in allaying anxiety,
reducing itching, and improving sleep patterns. Barbiturates

displaced bromides as the preferred sedative, and now these have been displaced by newer drugs termed 'tranquillisers'. Despite these advances the ideal sedative or tranquilliser, which would diminish tension and anxiety without disturbing alertness and being habit-forming, does not exist. Minor tranquillisers that are useful include Chlordiazepoxide (Librium); Diazepam (Valium); and Oxazepam (Serepax).

Depressive states often masquerade as anxiety or as skin problems. More commonly, depression will accompany or complicate itching disorders. In either case, the depression often requires treatment.

There are two main groups of anti-depressant drugs. One group, known as the monoamine oxidase inhibitors, are used almost exclusively by psychiatrists. Those most commonly used by other doctors are the tricyclic group. These include Doxepin (Sinequan, Deptran); Imipramine (Imiprin, Tofranil); Nortriptyline (Aventyl, Allegron); Amitriptyline (Tryptanol, Elavil) and Trimipramine (Surmontil), Dothiepin (Prothiadine). As mentioned previously, these drugs also have a very useful H_2-blocking anti-histamine effect.

The management of a patient with any chronic or itching skin condition requires skill in superficial psychotherapy. The greater the doctor's skill, the less he or she will have to rely on drugs. When they are needed, they should be used selectively for a defined period. There is a danger however, partly due to consumer resistance, with backing from the media, that rejection of these drugs may result in patients needlessly prolonging their disease and their discomfort.

CORTISONE AND THE SKIN

The various cortisone creams are the most common preparations recommended by the medical profession for use on the skin. They are known as topical corticosteroids: 'topical' because they are applied rather than taken by mouth; 'corticosteroids' (sometimes known simply as steroids) because they are derived from the natural hormone produced by the adrenal gland known as adrenal corticosteroid. Their history goes back a quarter of a century to 1952, when Dr Sulzberger, in the United States, first used hydrocortisone. Since then, various molecular changes have been made, often by the addition of fluorine to the basic structure. This has resulted in the increased activity, or the increased efficacy, of the subsequent preparation.

As a result of intense research, many topical corticosteroids have been developed that have remarkably beneficial effects. Their precise chemical structure determines their ability to affect various skin conditions. This is termed their potency. Other factors, however, are also relevant to their effectiveness. These include the vehicle or base in which the corticosteroid is carried. For example, ointments appear to be better absorbed than creams. Likewise, creams tend to be more effective than lotions, and so forth.

The age of the patient is also most important, since it determines the absorption capacity of the skin. The relative thinness of the infant's or young child's skin, combined with its large surface area in relation to body weight, tends to enhance the preparation's absorption capacity considerably. Similarly, the thinner, more fragile skin of the elderly tends to absorb more freely than does the thicker skin of middle-aged people.

There is also variation of absorption potential over the body's skin area. For instance, sites that have thinner skin—such as the eyelids—absorb better than areas of thicker skin such as the soles of the feet. The vascularity or blood supply of the area involved is also important in facilitating absorption. Consequently, the scrotum or face absorbs very freely. Opposing skin surfaces such as are found in the armpits or the groin area likewise increase the absorption potential of the preparation used.

The frequency of application is also critical, optimal results usually being achieved with two or perhaps three applications daily. If the preparation is applied too frequently, or for too long a period, there is a slowing down of responsiveness to it. Hence it is wise to change the type of preparation used fairly frequently, as the skin may become accustomed to, and subsequently resistant to, the frequent application of the same corticosteroid.

The topical application of corticosteroids has made possible the relief of much discomfort and disfigurement from chronic skin disease. As with all treatment, there are possible side-effects, but these are easily outweighed by the tremendous benefit their judicious use can offer.

Cortisone preparations achieve their effect by a strong anti-inflammatory action, whether the cause of the skin disorder be mechanical, chemical, microbiological, or immunological. They also have a strong immuno-suppressive action, and consequently diminish local anti-body production. Finally, they have an anti-mitotic effect on human skin. This accounts for their effect of slowing down the abnormal cell formation in the various scaling skin disorders.

Before using a corticosteroid preparation, two important factors must be considered. The first and foremost is the diagnosis. It is most important for the diagnosis to be correct, since while cortisone may suit one skin condition, it may have an adverse reaction on another very similar condition. Any confusion in this regard could have drastic consequences. The conditions most responsive to topical corticosteroids are:

- atopic eczema—flexural, discoid, dyshidrotic
- contact dermatitis—allergic, irritant
- neurodermatitis
- varicose eczema
- seborrhoeic eczema
- psoriasis.

Adverse reactions to the use of topical corticosteroid are seen in the following conditions:

- acne—adolescent, rosacea
- infections—bacterial, viral, fungal, parasitic
- leg ulcers.

The second factor to consider is which preparation to use. Obviously the best principle is to use hydrocortisone (the mildest steroid) where possible, or a stronger fluorinated compound in its lowest effective concentration. (Fluorinated corticosteroids should, however, be avoided in more sensitive areas such as the face or creases.) The chosen preparation should be applied to the smallest possible area for the shortest period of time.

What are the possible side-effects of using topical corticosteroids? They are primarily local, and may take many forms. Thinning of the skin may occur, with resultant striae or stretch marks appearing as purple or white streaks, particularly in the creases. The skin may also appear aged, with the blood vessels and superficial haemorrhages visible through the more transparent skin, particularly on the face.

There may be delayed healing of wounds, particularly when the preparation is used on varicose ulcers. Various infections, such as tinea, herpes and thrush, will be aggravated and the underlying disorder may become masked. Allergies to the preservative, stabiliser or perfume in the preparation may occur. If it also contains an antibiotic, this is again more likely to cause allergy problems.

The use of these preparations for facial acne may aggravate the acne, and cause secondary infections as well. Increased facial hair and depigmentation of the skin may also result. Furthermore, if the preparations are used in or too close to the eye, glaucoma, cataract, or activation of corneal herpes simplex may result.

Although theoretically possible, it is extremely rare for topical preparations to be absorbed in large enough amounts to have any significant internal side-effect. The only possible exception is when excessive amounts of strong preparations are used over large areas of a child's skin for long periods. For most adult patients, who use less than thirty grams of potent corticosteroid a day on less than one-third of the body, there is little evidence of significant internal side-effects (even with plastic occlusion—which increases absorption tenfold—overnight). Furthermore, the only known side-effect, that of diminishing the body's own corticosteroid production, is completely reversible within two to three days, should it occur.

The likelihood of internal side-effects may be diminished by the appropriate choice of the weakest effective preparation. Similarly, only small amounts of the chosen preparation should be used, and then only when and where necessary. The extent of the area of skin treated is most important, particularly with babies. Occlusive dressings to enhance absorption in thick areas of the skin should not be used over large areas for long periods of time.

Local side-effects may be prevented by using the appropriate-strength preparation for as short a period as possible. Small quantities of a preparation are often sufficient besides being more economical, and it is useful to be shown the correct amount to use. For example, a matchhead amount will adequately cover the back of the hand. It is also inadvisable to use these preparations more than twice or possibly three times a day, because the skin has a tendency to become resistant to their use, as well as the possibility of over-use.

Once the condition is under control, a less potent preparation should be used for maintenance. Where possible, alternative compounds (for example, tar preparations with eczema or dithranol with psoriasis) should replace, or alternate with, the corticosteroids. Once the condition has healed, then treatment should be gradually tapered off, to avoid a rebound.

Let me emphasise, however, that although we should be aware of the possible complications of using corticosteroids, this should not deter us from using them. Under careful supervision it is possible to use small quantities of potent preparations for short periods in complete safety, even on the face and creases. Many patients have benefited enormously from their use, and there is no real justification for being left with an uncomfortable, unsightly yet treatable condition because of unwarranted fears of side-effects.

7

Save your skin

Soaking up the sun's rays is one of life's great pleasures. Not only does a bright, sunny day warm us, but it makes us feel happy and provides the ideal atmosphere for pursuing many activities, including outdoor sports, walking, gardening, picnicking or just relaxing. Sunlight can also provide therapeutic and psychological benefits. It may relieve some of the symptoms of persons with arthritis, and certain skin diseases. Others believe that a bronzed body symbolises attractiveness, fitness and 'the good life'. Certainly, a small amount of sunlight is essential for normal, healthy bone growth by producing vitamin D in the skin. To be without sunlight would be to exist without one of the great pleasures in life. However, as with most enjoyable things, overindulgence may result in severe and irreversible damage. In fact if it were no longer fashionable to be tanned and people realised that tanning was by no means a harmless procedure, then dermatologists would lose a quarter of their patients, and beauty salons more than half their clients.

THE SUN

For the Egyptians, the sun was the great god Ra, whom they worshipped. Subsequent civilisations along the Mediterranean avoided the sun around the middle of the day, having a sleep indoors instead, and working later in the evening. Throughout most of the 19th century in Europe, pale skin was considered most attractive and very desirable. Tanned skin was vulgar—indicative of outdoor labour. However following the Industrial Revolution, pale skin began to be associated with unhealthy factory working conditions. Gradually, a sun tan became associated with a higher social status indicative of the non-working class. Later in the 19th century it again became fashionable to be pale and draped in Victorian protective clothing. This all changed again in the 20th century, possibly due to the vogue for 'heliotherapy', or sunlight treatment, for tuberculosis. A sun tan was then perceived as healthy, whereas pallor suggested tuberculosis, or at least poor health. Fashion leaders like Coco Chanel popularised 'le sun tan'. Chanel in particular achieved this by emerging, after a cruise on the Duke of Westminster's yacht, sporting a white suit and a deep brown tan. Unfortunately, research has shown that a sun tan is still considered attractive, healthy and even protective for the skin.

The sun is really a powerful star made up of gases at an incredible surface temperature of 6000° Celsius. Although it is 150 million kilometres away from the earth its vast energy, in the form of electromagnetic radiation, reaches us in one minute. Outside the earth's atmosphere, direct exposure to sunlight would be fatal, due to the lethal effect on living cells of large doses of X, gamma and short ultraviolet rays. Fortunately, we are protected by the absorbing or scattering effect of dust particles, moisture droplets, and ozone in the atmosphere.

The electromagnetic energy coming from the sun is comprised of a wide range of radiation which may be arranged according to wavelengths, which are measured in nanometers (nm). This radiation includes X-rays, which are the shortest, and ranges through gamma rays, ultraviolet rays, visible light and infrared waves to radiowaves, which are the longest. Most of this radiation is in the form of X, gamma and short ultraviolet rays, which fortunately never reach the Earth.

Ultraviolet rays range between 200 and 400 nm. UVC below 290 nm is filtered out before reaching us, and we are left with the suntan-bequeathing radiation UVB and UVA, which makes up less than 1 per cent of the total solar energy. UVB (290–320 nm)

SPECTRUM OF SOLAR RADIATION

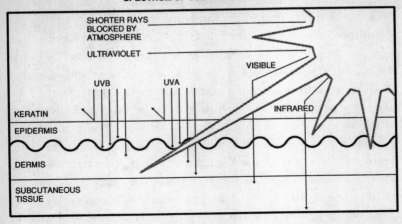

is a slightly shorter wavelength than UVA (320–400 nm), and therefore does not penetrate the skin as deeply. Visible light, a longer wavelength again, penetrates even more deeply than UVA (its ability to penetrate the skin can be seen by shining a torch through the skin of the webs between the fingers). Sunlight, as we receive it, consists more of visible light and infrared radiation than ultraviolet radiation, but these effect our skin also.

A number of variables affect the strength of sunlight. These include:

1. Latitude: Sunlight increases in strength with decreasing latitude as we approach the equator. This is because the ozone layer is thinner over the equator.

2. Altitude: Due to less filtering at increased altitude, sunlight strength increases with height.

3. Seasons: Summer sunlight is stronger than winter sunlight.

4. Time of day: The lower the angle of the sun above the horizon, the greater the atmospheric distance which must be crossed. Therefore, at noon in summer, with the sun almost directly overhead, the sunlight is most intense. About 60 per cent of the total UV radiation is received between 11 am and 3 pm, summer time.

5. Cloud or pollution: The more clouds or pollution in the atmosphere, the more sunlight will be reflected off and the less received at the earth's surface.

6. Stratospheric ozone: The earth's ozone layer is a layer of ozone gas high in the upper atmosphere that plays a major role in the absorption of UV radiation. It filters out most of the UVA and UVB radiation, and *all* of the UVC. With decreasing ozone levels, increasing radiation will be received at the earth's surface. The normal thickness of the ozone layer varies. For instance, the layer is thinner over the tropics. Consequently, the intensity of UV radiation is approximately 15 per cent greater there than elsewhere. The thickness of the ozone layer also varies with the seasons. It is thickest in winter, so the effects of sunlight are more intense during the summer months.

Localised episodic reduction in ozone has been seen, particularly in spring, during the last ten years, over Antarctica, with gradual global depletion over some years. The ozone 'hole' that hovered over Australia for three weeks in December, 1987, gave an equivalent UV dose to three weeks on the Queensland coast in mid summer. It is estimated that a 1 per cent depletion in the stratospheric ozone layer results in a 2 per cent increase in UVB at the earth's surface, and therefore a 4 per cent increase in the number of skin cancers. This would mean an increase of about 5000 skin cancers, with an additional five to six deaths per year from non-melanoma cancer and ten to fifteen from melanoma. This ozone depletion also results in diminished immunological protection, so that the likelihood of developing more severe fungal and viral infections, as well as cancer, is much greater.

SKIN TYPE AND SUN SUSCEPTIBILITY

Susceptibility to sun-induced damage also depends on one's skin type. This is largely governed by the amount of pigment in the skin, and one's ancestry. Those individuals with a darker skin have more protection than those with a fair skin. Similarly, those with skins that tan easily are more protected than those who burn rather than tan. Races with a black or brown skin are much less likely to suffer from sunlight-induced problems than the Caucasians, with their light-coloured skin; they are certainly not exempt, however, from the damaging effects of prolonged sun exposure.

One's ethnic origins therefore are most important in assessing the skin's response to prolonged sun exposure. People of Celtic origin are statistically much more prone to irreversible sun damage. These light-complexioned people, who are descendants of the Celtic natives of Britain, Scotland, Ireland and northern France, appear to have some biological defect which interferes with normal pigment production and the repair of sun-induced damage. Even amongst Celts, though, those who are blue-eyed and have a lighter complexion, red or blond hair and freckled skin, are more susceptible to sun damage than darker individuals.

Recent research conducted in Australia by the Anti-Cancer Council has revealed an interesting tendency. It appears that the skin-cancer risk is low amongst British migrants who arrived in Australia after the age of 20 years—even those who work outdoors and have lived in Australia for decades. By comparison, those who migrated before the age of 20 years have a higher incidence of skin cancer, which increases with age and eventually exceeds that of the Australian-born population.

Although the risk of skin cancer is related to cumulative lifetime exposure to UV radiation, it is the type of skin that children have, together with more leisure time spent outdoors, that is critical. On average, children and adolescents receive three times more UV radiation than adults do, and more than 50 per cent of lifetime exposure may be gained at this time. Nevertheless, continued adult exposure is still very significant.

THE DANGERS OF SOLARIUMS

The promotion of tanning has been a big business. In our society a good sun tan is equated with health, success and sexual desirability. 'Soft Sun', 'Dr X's Solarium', and 'Safe Sun' are just some of the reassuring terms used to describe the booming business of tanning bodies. Solarium franchises have been a lucrative business in both the United States and Australia. Unfortunately, however, it is the people of these two countries whose skin is least able to tolerate the extra radiation. In fact the UVA units originally came from Europe, and Germany in particular, where there is much less environmental sunshine, and it is less intense; furthermore, in Europe these units are primarily promoted for private home use, not public use in tanning parlours, beauty salons, hairdressing salons, gymnasiums, etc. This means that in addition to their potential harmful effect being greatly diminished, far fewer people are at risk.

The artificial light sources used in the solariums are usually fluorescent tubes emitting mainly UVA wavelengths. However, it is impossible for them to be totally confined to this wavelength as a continuous spectrum is emitted, and at least 2 per cent of the wavelength will be in the UVB band. Tanning is usually carried out on a bed-like apparatus with either half or total body exposure possible; exposure times are long, therefore stand-up arrangements are less practical.

Exposure of the average Caucasian skin to UVA solariums will produce tanning within about ten minutes, with the maximum tanning being reached in about an hour. Burning, although certainly possible, is unlikely. The acquired tan is, however, short lived, and requires regular frequent exposures to maintain it. UVB solariums are much more likely to cause burning, but the tan they produce is the so-called 'true or delayed tan', which is associated with new melanin formation, and consequently is longer lasting. It is, however, important to be aware that although a tan protects against UVB sunburn, it does not protect the skin from the cancer-producing or premature ageing effects of UVA radiation. This is because, in order to tan, some epidermal and dermal damage must occur.

There are numerous dangers associated with solariums:

1. UVA penetrates deeper than UVB, so most of the damage occurs in the dermis, to the supportive structures, resulting in severe and premature photo-ageing.
2. It is quite unnatural for the skin to be exposed to more UVA

than UVB; this compounds the effect of UVB, causing more severe and permanent damage to the superficial skin layers, resulting in skin cancer.

3. Exposure occurs over a larger body area than normal, for a longer period of time, and more frequently. Therefore damage is more intense and cumulative. This results in damage to the body's immune system, allowing skin cancers to develop and progress in an uncontrolled manner.

4. UVA doesn't cause a 'sunburn', which is Nature's warning of excessive exposure. This absence of discomfort allows you to accumulate far more damage than if you were exposed to sunlight.

5. With UVA, photo-allergic reactions are very common. These may be caused by various soaps, perfumes and cosmetics. Many common tablets can cause these severe skin reactions also. They include some antibiotics, diuretics, tranquillisers, anti-diabetic drugs and the birth control pill.

6. The long UVA rays are able to penetrate the eyelid, ending up in the lens of the eye. Here they cause cataracts to develop. Cataracts are the second most common cause of blindness in the USA and Australia.

Misleading advertising of solariums is commonplace. Various advertising brochures present different inaccuracies. There are, however, three fundamental inaccuracies which most of them contain.

The first is the claim made for the enormous benefits of UVA radiation for the body! They reject the 'blazing and potentially dangerous sun', only to promote 'the rich golden tan, which gives you that healthy, confident, affluent look'. Who could resist, especially as they say that the radiation which produces a tan is also the major source of vitamin D? In fact, the major source of vitamin D is dairy products and fish oils, not sunlight. Moreover, such supplementation of vitamin D is hardly necessary in our society: vitamin D deficiency results in rickets, a virtually non-existent condition in developed countries. Ironically, many such tanning units are found in gymnasiums and health clubs, although they emit about the most unhealthy rays possible for the skin.

The second misleading claim concerns the safety of these units. Brochures maintain that they 'filter out the potentially harmful part of the UV range', and use only the 'beneficial tanning rays'. Some even state that they produce 'a safe tan, without drying and prematurely ageing the skin', and further, that such a tan is 'a very effective measure towards the prevention of skin cancer'.

Thirdly, they state that: 'it is not necessary to wear protective goggles'—despite increasing evidence of cataract formation.

Clearly, tanning for cosmetic purposes is not a harmless procedure. This is equally true whether the tan is developed by lying on sunny beaches or frequenting solariums. The greatest disadvantage of the solarium concept is that it allows people to maintain a tan all the year round. Such people thus have the means of accumulating consistent cellular damage, resulting eventually in tissue breakdown which manifests itself as premature ageing and cancer.

The widespread use of solariums is a public health issue, just as smoking has become. In the United States the Government Department of Health and Human Services, together with the Food and Drug Administration, is very much aware of the danger involved in the indiscriminate use of solariums. As a result, regulations governing their use and their equipment are being enforced. All operators are required to be licensed, and their equipment regularly calibrated and checked. Posters must be prominently displayed, warning of the skin and eye dangers, and referring to the various drugs and diseases which may adversely affect the client using the solarium; and finally a consent form must be signed. The problem in a free country is that entrepreneurs can start almost any business they want, as long as it doesn't obviously harm anybody. But the law governing gradual harm, showing up years later, is quite unclear.

THE EFFECTS OF SUNLIGHT

The effects of sunlight are due not only to UV radiation A and B, but also to infrared waves (heat) and visible light. These latter rays have recently been shown to both activate and augment the effect of the ultraviolet. The effect of sunlight is cumulative—like smoking and lung damage, or excessive alcohol and liver disease. Nothing much happens initially but after a lag period of ten to twenty years major problems may arise. Caucasians, particularly of Celtic stock, living in Australia are the most susceptible.

1. SUNBURN

The effect of acute sun damage, either due to overexposure or minor exposure of inappropriate skin type, is known as sunburn. This is inflammation of the skin due to an overdose of UV radiation. UVB is the major component causing such burning and later tanning. Sunburn may vary from mild redness of the skin to swelling and blistering. Rarely, a high temperature may result and circulatory collapse occur. This degree of radiation burn will injure skin cells. As a result, the DNA in the cell nucleus will be damaged, resulting in reduced function of immune cells and often cell death. The long-term effect of this is the development of skin cancer and premature photo-ageing.

2. TANNING

This is also a short-term effect of sunlight exposure. Melanin, the pigment protein, is formed in specialised cells found in the basal layer (growth area) of the epidermis. This melanin, which is what gives skin its colouring, also protects it to a certain extent from sunburn, by absorbing sunlight. It does not, however, protect the skin from chronic sun exposure, which may result in serious damage. Initially after exposure, immediate tanning occurs. This is transient and is due to oxidation of the skin's existing melanin. It is produced mainly by UVA radiation. True tanning takes much longer, but may persist for weeks and involves the formation of new melanin. This is mainly produced by UVB. The amount produced depends on racial and genetic factors.

A tan does not protect the skin from further damage, nor is it necessary for good health. It is, in fact, the skin's response to repeated radiation injury and is therefore a sign of skin damage. Tanning is merely a fashion that hopefully will come to be regarded as outdated.

3. ALLERGIES

Sun allergies, or photosensitivity, are not uncommon. These reactions occur after only short periods of exposure to sunlight. They may appear as red blotches, raised bumps, hives or blisters on exposed skin. They may be due to previous sensitisation of the skin to sunlight and will usually occur at about the same time each summer. Other reactions may be caused by contact with certain potential sensitisers such as some soaps, creams, perfumes or plants. Various drugs may cause these allergies also: some antibiotics, diuretics, tranquillisers, anti-diabetic tablets and the birth control pill, for example.

4. DISEASES

Some specific diseases are precipitated or aggravated by sunlight. More common ones include herpes simplex (cold sores) and chicken pox. Rarer diseases include various collagen disorders such as lupus erythematosus.

5. PREMATURE AGEING

This is mainly caused by UVA and some UVB penetrating the deeper layers of the skin (dermis) and damaging the support structures and diminishing the immune function of the cells. The familiar changes discussed in detail elsewhere include:

- thinning of the skin
- thickening of the skin
- increased pigmentation
- decreased pigmentation
- 'broken capillaries'.

Of course premature ageing increases with age, but more particularly with exposure to sunlight. Consequently, Australians generally photo-age many years earlier than their European contemporaries.

6. SOLAR KERATOSES ('SUN SPOTS')

A solar keratosis is one of the commonest manifestations of excessive sun exposure. The word solar means sun, and keratosis means scaling, so solar keratoses are often called 'sun spots'. They most commonly occur in people of Celtic background, with fair skin, outdoor workers and those who have lived in Australia for most of their lives. The areas exposed are the most commonly affected—the hands, forearms, face, ears and neck. Approximately 50 per cent of people aged over 40 years living in Australia are affected. Solar keratoses are not skin cancers but are considered pre-cancerous or as having a premalignant potential in the epidermis. Occasionally they may progress to become malignant, although this is not common (only about 1 per cent). However, they indicate that sufficient sunlight exposure has been accumulated for the possible development of other skin cancers. If you like, they are a sunlight meter, and people who have developed them need to be carefully examined for evidence of skin cancer.

Features

Solar keratoses appear as small, rough patches on the skin's surface. They vary in colour from skin colour to red or brown. They are scaly, and although the scale may fall off it usually reappears. Very occasionally they may fall off and not reappear. Usually they are tender and bleed if knocked, and may sting on exposure to sunlight. Their size may vary from pinpoints to quite large horny protuberances. Thickening of the base of the lesion, with increasing redness and tenderness, indicates activity and the possibility of malignant change.

Treatment

1. *Cryotherapy*: This is the use of extreme cold to snap freeze the spot. Either liquid nitrogen (-196°C) or solid carbon dioxide (-79°C) is applied, using either a cotton applicator or a spray. The freezing of the tissue causes rapid cell death and destruction of the spot. This treatment creates a small blister under the spot which then dries up and falls off within two weeks. Scarring does not usually occur.

2. *Diathermy or cautery*: This is the use of heat to burn the spot. An electric needle is applied to the spot after the area has been

deadened with a local anaesthetic. The heat produced by the high-amperage, low-voltage current causes cell death. Healing may take two to three weeks, and a small scar may be left. This method may be used for larger or thicker spots.

3. *Chemotherapy*: An anti-cancer drug, 5-Fluorouracil, may be applied in the form of a cream or lotion, twice daily for three weeks. Wherever solar keratoses or other solar damage is present, acute inflammation followed by superficial erosion will occur. The treated area will become red and sore, but heal within two to three weeks without scarring. This method is used only if very large numbers of solar keratoses are present.

4. *Surgery*: Occasionally, when the diagnosis is uncertain or the spot is very large, it may need to be excised—that is, surgically removed. This is done under a local anaesthetic and the piece removed and examined microscopically by a pathologist—otherwise known as a biopsy. Most commonly a shave excision would be used, although sometimes excision and suturing would be performed.

SKIN CANCER

Skin cancer is by far the most serious result of sun damage to the skin. Sun exposure is not the only cause of skin cancer. It can also be produced by chronic irritation of the skin. In England, in 1775, Dr Percival Pott described cancer of the scrotum in chimneysweeps, which was caused by soot. Natives of the northern Himalayas who carry canisters of hot charcoal next to the skin of their abdomens to keep warm, develop cancer in this area. However in Australia, sun-exposed areas of skin commonly develop skin cancer.

The word 'carcinogen' has become all too familiar in recent years. A carcinogen is something that causes cancer. In our society, sunlight is the most common carcinogen, since it is the leading cause of skin cancer, the most common form of all cancers. Skin cancer is predominantly caused by chronic cell injury induced by prolonged exposure to infrared and ultraviolet radiation. There is usually, however, quite a long latent period or delay between the exposure to solar radiation and the appearance of skin cancer. The energy from this UVA and UVB radiation is absorbed at various levels of the epidermis, causing cellular damage. Most of the damage occurs in the genetic material known as DNA that enables cells to duplicate themselves. In most cases, a cell manages to repair this damage. Eventually, though, it may not be able to do so, in which case the cell may die, contributing to the appearance of premature skin ageing; or it may change its character completely. Such changes in cells are called mutations, and some of these mutations may be cancerous, and then grow out of control. At the same time, the body's immune surveillance system has also been impaired by cumulative sun damage. Consequently, these abnormal cells are unable to be checked or removed by the body and so they continue to grow out of control, also spreading to other parts of the body.

Incidence

The relationship between the incidence of skin cancer and exposure to sunlight has been firmly established. First, skin cancers are more prevalent on those areas most continuously exposed to the sun, such as the face and hands. Second, the overall incidence of skin cancers is much higher in those areas of the world where there are many months of high-intensity solar radiation and a tradition of sunbathing. Third, skin cancer mainly affects a fair-skinned population. These people are genetically prone to develop skin cancer. Persons with blue or green eyes, fair or red hair, and pale skin—notably Irish and other Celtic peoples—are especially vulnerable. Ireland has the world's highest skin-cancer death rate after South Africa and Australia, even though Ireland is in a latitude that receives less than half the ultraviolet radiation of either of the other countries. The overall incidence of cancer amongst Caucasians in the United States is fifteen times greater than for blacks. For predisposed individuals of Celtic ancestry, living in potentially sun-intense countries such as the United States, South Africa and Australia, skin cancer is a real hazard, although there is a considerable period of latency between the time of damage and the appearance of the consequences. This may, in fact, range from ten to thirty years. Lastly, the incidence of skin cancer has increased with the amount of leisure time available, and also since a sun tan has been considered a status symbol, and therefore fashionable.

Skin-cancer rates in Australia are higher than anywhere else in the world. It is the most common form of cancer in Australia, affecting all age groups from adolescents upwards. About 140 000 Australians develop skin cancer each year. In fact, between 2 and 3 per cent of the population over 40 years of age have skin cancer and may be unaware of it. This means that two of every three Australians will develop some form of skin cancer in their lifetime, and 1000 will die of it each year. Of these deaths, 800 will be from a melanoma and 200 from non-melanoma skin cancer. Unfortunately, the incidence rate of all skin cancers is still rising at a rapid rate, though it is hoped this will change, due to the activity of public health bodies such as the various State Cancer Councils, and improved public awareness.

The cost to all Australians of this skin cancer 'epidemic' is very high. Professor McCarthy of the Sydney Melanoma Unit has estimated the cost of treatment to be about $100 million per year. If you add to this work days lost and the cost of preventative measures such as sun-protection, sun screens and advertising campaigns—a more realistic figure would be $400–500 million per year! Yet skin cancer is largely a preventable disease.

Skin cancer, like all cancers, is marked by the uncontrolled growth of certain cells. There are three common forms of skin cancer, named according to the cells from which they develop. The most common is the basal cell carcinoma (BCC), which rarely spreads to other tissues. The next most common is the squamous cell carcinoma (SCC), which may spread or metastasise, and may arise from a pre-cancerous lesion known as a solar keratosis. Finally, there is the highly dangerous melanoma.

BASAL CELL CARCINOMA

The BCC is a tumour arising from the cells of the basal layer of the epidermis. The abnormal cells leave their normal position and invade the dermis. It is a relatively innocent cancer, as it does not usually invade blood vessels and spread to distant sites. If left untreated, however, it will quietly spread to the surrounding skin and erode underlying tissues, such as bone. Hence, in the past, these cancers have been called 'rodent ulcers'. These tumours make up about 75 per cent of all skin cancers in Australia.

Causes

Unlike most SCCs, BCCs are not usually preceded by an obvious pre-malignant lesion. Although prolonged sunlight exposure is an important causal factor, other factors must also be involved. BCCs are much more common in sunny climates and in light-skinned individuals, and two-thirds occur on the head and neck. However, one-third occur in relatively protected sites, such as on the body, eyelids, and behind the ears. It is therefore thought that regional factors must also be involved.

Features

Patients often describe how they have noticed a spot which, although it is not troubling them, does not go away; it may bleed or crust over, but will never quite heal. The appearances are varied. Most typically, it is a small pearl-like nodule with fine blood vessels overlying it. Sometimes it looks like a very small erosion of the skin, or an ulcer. Overlying it, there may be a small crust. Occasionally it appears like a red scaly plaque with a scalloped margin.

SQUAMOUS CELL CARCINOMA

The SCC is a tumour arising from the squamous cells of the epidermis that lie above the basal layer. This form of cancer easily invades the dermis, and may on occasions spread to local lymph glands or more widely through the blood stream. These tumours make up about 20 per cent of all skin cancers in Australia.

Causes

SCCs are much more prevalent on sun-damaged skin. They may, however, arise following prolonged exposure to chemical carcinogens such as tar, lubricating oils, creosote and soot. Occasionally they arise at the site of an old injury, such as a burn or leg ulcer. The taking of arsenic for medical purposes, many years previously, will predispose one to developing a SCC. The majority of these cancers are due to the cumulative effect of solar damage in genetically predisposed people, and occur on sun-exposed areas. The incidence is high amongst outdoor workers—especially those with fair or freckled complexions—living in countries like Australia, South Africa, or in the US states of California or Florida. (The incidence is fifteen times less in blacks than in whites of the same area.)

Features

SCCs rarely arise in healthy-looking skin. They usually appear against a background of blotchy pigmentation, alternate thickening and thinning of the skin, and wrinkling. Frequently, they occur within a longstanding solar keratosis. The most common sites are the backs of the hands, the arms and the facial area.

The earliest sign of a SCC is often a firm thickening of the skin, usually at the base of a solar keratosis. More frequently, however, the earliest sign is a warty growth, or a small ulcer, with a rolled solid border. Initially the ulcer is not obvious because of a firmly adhering crust, which bleeds when it is knocked off. The lower lip is a favourite site for these SCCs. Here a SCC may be preceded by a white flat patch, known as leukoplakia, or dry, scaly, cracked lips. It may begin as a persistent fissure or crack, which becomes hard and ulcerated, or as a warty or fleshy, red growth.

MELANOMA

The melanoma is a malignant tumour of melanocytes, which are the melanin, or pigment-producing cells in the basal layer of the epidermis. It is the least common but most lethal form of skin cancer because of its potential to spread rapidly. Melanoma is unfortunately more common in Australia than in any other country of the world. Also, like other skin cancers, the frequency of melanoma appears to be increasing by about 7 per cent per year, which means a doubling every ten years. Melanomas make up about 5 per cent of all skin cancers in Australia, but cause 80 per cent of the 1000 deaths each year.

Causes

The complete cause of melanoma is unknown. However, several important observations throw some light on possible causative factors.

Genetic factors are clearly important. People of Celtic origin, particularly those with red hair, fair skin and blue eyes, are far more likely to develop melanoma, whereas the tumour is uncommon in black races. The tendency to freckle and burn rather than tan appears also to be related to the likelihood of developing melanoma. This impaired ability to produce an even tan, but rather freckles, results in poor protection against UV radiation. Remember, it is not the tan itself which protects, but more the ability to tan.

Hormonal factors play a role since women are twice as likely as men to develop melanoma, although their chance of cure is also higher than it is for males. They also appear more commonly on the backs of men and the legs of women. Furthermore, the tumour is exceedingly rare before puberty.

Environment is obviously relevant. Melanoma is more common in Australia and the southern states of North America, with their long hours of annual sunlight, and is twice as common in Queensland as in Tasmania. There is considerable evidence, therefore, that prolonged exposure to sunlight plays a central role in determining the frequency of melanoma. The closer to the Equator, the higher the incidence. The earth's surface is partially protected from the sun's ionising radiation by a layer of ozone. This ozone layer is thinnest at the Equator and thickest at the Poles. Over recent years it has, however, been decreasing in thickness, as previously discussed, and there has been a concomitant increase in the number of melanomas.

Lifestyle also plays a role. Melanomas are much more common amongst people who are exposed to sunlight intermittently, such as on holidays, than amongst outdoor workers who have more continous exposure. This is particularly so if they sunburn before tanning during childhood or adolescence.

The body's immune response is critical. UV radiation, passing through the skin into the cells of the epidermis, damages the DNA in the cell's nucleus, causing abnormal behaviour of the cell, resulting in malignancy. Normally, the body's immune surveillance system will identify these damaged cells and dispose of them. UV radiation, however, also damages those cells responsible for this immune response, in particular the Langerhans cells of the epidermis. With chronic sun exposure, their numbers decrease dramatically and their ability to act effectively is also impaired. Thus we find that the immune system is suppressed by UV radiation, allowing damaged cells to grow unchecked. This may account for the higher frequency of melanoma in relatively non-exposed sites, such as on the back. It also means that it is never too late to start taking precautions to allow the immune system to recover, thereby allowing further protection against cancer.

Moles are important. Most adults have about twenty to twenty-five moles on their bodies. Research has shown that the more moles present, the more likely you are to develop a melanoma. Some people have a tendency to develop unusual moles known as dysplastic moles, and are then at a greater risk of developing a melanoma. This variety of mole is usually quite large, only slightly raised, with marked colour variation and an irregular border or lop-sided shape. They can occur singly or be multiple. However, only about a third of melanomas occur in association with a mole, therefore two-thirds develop as a brand new spot.

Features

Melanomas may vary considerably in appearance. Most—in fact 60 per cent—appear suddenly, without warning, and are symptom-free. In the early stages they usually look like an unusual freckle, appearing in a relatively unexposed site. Their specific features include:

1. *Asymmetry*, or a lop-sided shape.
2. *Borders* that are usually irregular and the edges poorly defined.

3. *Colour* that varies through shades of tan, brown and black, although red, white and blue may also be present.
4. *Diameter* often greater than six millimetres (or the size of the top of a pencil).
5. *Elevation* that may be obvious or quite subtle.

Suspicious mole changes

Other melanomas, only 30 per cent in fact, will arise in, or near, a pre-existing mole. Any significant—that is obvious—change in a mole should be noted. Some of the changes you may observe in a mole that should arouse suspicion include:

Colour: becoming darker or more variable.
Size: becoming wider or raised.
Shape: becoming asymmetrical or border irregular.
Surface: becoming rough or ulcerated.
Sensation: becoming itchy or painful.

Early detection and adequate treatment results in a very good cure rate of over 90 per cent. If you notice any of these changes on your skin you should consult a dermatologist immediately. The change may not be dangerous but quite normal; however, if it is uncertain, a biopsy will be recommended. If your doctor suggests a biopsy of a suspicious mole, do not hesitate to have this done. It does not affect the course of the tumour, whether the biopsy is partial or complete. The important thing is to act quickly. When such changes as mentioned above are heeded and medical attention sought, the prognosis is infinitely better than if they go unrecognised or are ignored.

If we do not change our habit of sun worship, it has been predicted that about 1 of every 100 people born in the year 2000 will develop a melanoma during their lifetime. A wide range of factors, including a longer life span, increased leisure time, the fashion for more exposed skin and depletion of the ozone layer, will have contributed to this increase.

THE ABC OF SPOTTING DANGER

*The ABCDE system can help you detect signs of trouble early on
while they are almost 100 per cent curable.
The illustrations below show moles on their way to melanoma. Watch for:*

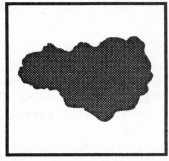

A *symmetry; one half of the mole is
unlike the other*

B *order irregularity, scalloped
or poorly defined edges*

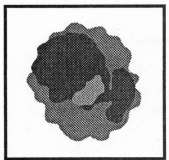

C *olor variations, inconsistency,
tan brown, black, red, white, or
even blue*

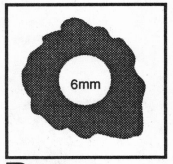

D *iameter, larger than a pencil*

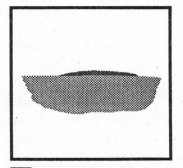

E *levation, may be obvious or subtle*

125

TREATMENT OF SKIN CANCER

Prevention

Prevention is the key to eradicating skin cancer. This basically means protection from sunlight and early diagnosis. Some protection should commence in childhood, and so primarily is the responsibility of parents and teachers. It has been shown that most sun damage, estimated at 50 per cent, occurs during childhood and adolescence. However, as the damage is cumulative, adult sun exposure contributes to the overall dosage or damage accumulated. Once a critical dose has been obtained, a cancer will be triggered.

Natural protection is the simplest and best. This means avoiding sunlight around the middle of the day, and creating or seeking out shade. Broad-brimmed or Legionnaire-style hats and adequate light clothing can also provide shade.

Sun screens are a very important form of protection. They should be used on a daily basis throughout the summer months. The

FOUR STEPS TO SUN PROTECTION

Stay out of the sun in the middle of the day.

Use sun block SPF 15 or higher.

Cover up with a t-shirt and a hat.

Make sure children know how important it is to cover up.

product you use must be SPF 15+, which means that it is broad spectrum and therefore effective against both UVA and UVB radiation. Whether it is a cream, milk or lotion is a personal preference. If the product stings the eyes with sweating, then a lotion, which is better absorbed, may be preferable. However, lotions should be applied to dry skin and at least fifteen minutes before sun exposure, so that they are properly absorbed by the skin and thus able to afford adequate protection. Even water-resistant products should be re-applied after prolonged swimming. This routine should commence in childhood, particularly as children spend many hours playing outside, especially in the middle of the day. Even if they wear a hat, much light is reflected onto the skin from pavements and walls, causing skin damage. This can only be prevented by adequate sun screens applied before going to school, and preferably again at lunch time. This habit must become as natural as cleaning teeth and combing hair!

Adults also must routinely apply sun screens in the summer months because they are unlikely to wear a hat to hang out the washing or drive the car. In fact, much sun damage is acquired through the window glass of cars, resulting in cancers appearing more frequently on the right side of the face and right arm and hand in Australia, whereas the opposite applies in the USA. We must become aware that sun damage is acquired gradually but daily, and not just at weekends or during recreational activity. Consequently, sun screens for adults should also be a daily routine, even under make-up. Even when wearing a hat it is advisable to have a sun screen on to block reflected light from buildings, sand or snow.

Regular self-examination is a useful method for ensuring the early detection of melanoma and other skin cancers. I recommend that people at risk institute a regular three-monthly program of self-examination. To do this you must first become familiar with your skin and your pattern of moles, freckles and 'beauty marks'. Be alert to changes in the number, size, shape and colour of pigmented areas. If you notice new spots, or any rapid or obvious changes in existing ones, you should ask to see a dermatologist. If you are uncertain whether a mole is enlarging, you could mark its outline on tracing paper. Then, two months later, retrace it, to see if there has been a change. Spots that are detected and treated in the early stages are almost always curable.

The following is a suggested method of self-examination that will ensure that no area of the body is neglected. To perform this you will need a full-length mirror, a hand mirror and a brightly lit room. This step-by-step method, if done every three months, will provide you with an 'early warning system' against skin cancer.

Removal

The method used to treat skin cancer depends on a number of factors. These include the type of cancer, its size, its location, the patient's age and previous treatment and the expertise of the doctor. Frequently there is no single or ideal form of treatment for each tumour, so the option chosen depends on the doctor's experience. I shall describe some of the more commonly-used removal techniques, and the type of cancer they may be used on.

1. Carefully examine your torso, back and front, in the mirror. Check your sides, raising your arms.
2. Check your forearms, palms, and underarms, bending your elbow to look at the back.
3. Use a hand mirror to check your neck, upper back and scalp.
4. Go over your feet and legs, check your thighs, behind the knees and between toes.
5. Then examine the lower back and buttocks, again with the hand mirror to help you.

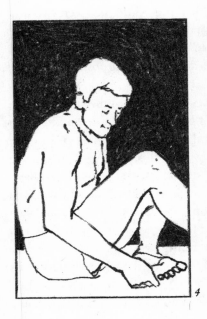

Cryotherapy: The only suitable cryogen (freezing agent) for skin cancers is liquid nitrogen because it is the coldest, at -196°C. Others, such as nitrous oxide (-90°C) and carbon dioxide (-79°C), do not achieve sufficient freezing at adequate tumour depth. The faster the freezing of the tissue, the more effective it is in causing cell death in the treatment area. Liquid nitrogen should therefore be sprayed directly onto the tumour and surrounding skin, until a rim of tissue of at least 0.5 centimetres is frozen around it. This frozen rim should last at least one minute before thawing occurs. After complete thawing, which may take approximately five minutes, the area should be refrozen, in the same manner. The depth of freezing equates with the time taken to achieve freezing: the freeze margin; and the time taken to thaw, as well as the number of repeat freeze-thaw cycles. This treatment is a relatively simple office procedure, not normally requiring local anaesthesia. The initial application is uncomfortable, with pain lasting only about one minute during the thawing phase. The following day a blister will form, and then a crust, with healing taking between two and six weeks. Very little scarring usually results from this treatment.

This method is mainly used to treat superficial BCCs, which are the commonest form of skin cancer. If the diagnosis is in doubt, a biopsy will precede the procedure.

Curettage: This technique involves scooping out the skin tumour. The method is suitable for small but thicker lesions, and allows samples to be sent for pathological examination. It is not suitable for areas prone to scarring, or the corners of the eye. This is also an office procedure, but local anaesthetic is used to make it painless. A spoon-shaped curette is used to scoop the tissue away. This curettage is done in all directions across the tumour, and the bleeding stopped by diathermy. The procedure is repeated two to three times to ensure that all malignant cells are removed. Sometimes the resultant area may be treated with cryotherapy as well, to ensure total tumour eradication. Healing usually takes two to six weeks, depending on the size and site of the tumour. Some scarring may result.

This method is mainly used to treat more nodular forms of BCC.

Excision: This is the preferred treatment for all tumours with the potential for metastatic spread, and recurrent tumours. Again, this is usually an office procedure performed under local anaesthesia. The tumour is excised as an ellipse, with a margin of 0.5 to one centimetre of skin around it, and the specimen is sent to pathology. The length of the ellipse must be at least three times its width to obtain easy closure. The gap is then sutured, and after five to ten days the sutures are removed. Occasionally, if wound closure is difficult, skin grafting may be necessary.

This method is used to treat all SCCs and melanomas, as well as any other tumours which may be recurrent, large or in awkward positions.

The treatment of melanoma is surgical excision. If the diagnosis is uncertain, this should be preceded by a biopsy. Local excision, with a clearance of at least one centimetre, is recommended for an early melanoma, less than a millimetre in thickness. Thicker lesions need wider excision, sometimes requiring a skin graft. Radical surgery, with associated lymph gland removal, is now rarely required because, with heightened awareness and early diagnosis, thinner tumours are being removed. If the tumour is less than a millimetre thick at removal, there is a greater than 90 per cent chance of a cure.

Sometimes more sophisticated and newer methods of treatment need to be used. These may include local perfusion of the limb with chemotherapy, or general chemotherapy for advanced melanoma. Cytotoxic agents in combination may be used, but tend to be very toxic. Much research is now under way to utilise the body's immune system to fight this particular type of cancer. Meanwhile, BCG vaccinations may be used to induce non-specific immune stimulation. A vaccine made from melanoma cells artificially infected with the vaccinia (smallpox) virus is being successfully trialled in patients who have had a deep melanoma excised. The vaccine appears to stimulate the patient's immunity to the melanoma and so help to prevent the cancer recurring. This may dramatically improve the survival rate of those who develop this potentially fatal disease.

Radiotherapy: Superficial X-ray therapy is an acceptable form of treatment of skin cancers, with some reservations. With the other forms of treatment available, this method is now much less commonly used. Several treatments are usually required, and it takes six to eight weeks for healing to occur. Radiotherapy is now mainly used on patients unsuitable for surgery, or on recurrent tumours. It is not usually recommended for patients other than the elderly, on sites of constant trauma, or in areas previously treated with radiotherapy.

Two new methods of treating skin cancer are now used in Australia:

Micrographic surgery: This technique involves excising the tumour under local anaesthetic in a manner that allows frozen-section examination of the entire cut surface of the specimen. Areas of incomplete excision can then be precisely identified on tissue-maps and then re-excised. This method is very time-consuming and specialised, and usually only used for recurrent BCCs and ones adjacent to vital structures, where tissue sparing is crucial.

Retinoids: These are synthetic derivatives of vitamin A. They have a powerful effect on the growth of epithelial cells and have been developed as a treatment for many skin diseases. Recently they have also been successfully used in the treatment of non-melanoma skin cancer. Taken by mouth, these drugs can control, and sometimes clear, skin cancer. Much research is progressing into these promising compounds.

8

An index of skin disorders

ACNE

Acne is a very common inflammatory disorder of the oil glands, or pilosebaceous follicles. The majority of these glands are confined to the face, chest and back, and they are most active during adolescence. The course of the disorder is variable, as is the age of onset. Usually it appears a little earlier in girls, but in either sex it is very uncommon before the age of 10. The duration of acne is as variable as the severity. In mild cases the condition may resolve itself spontaneously within a few months, but typically it will last for a year or two. If severe or if chronic, the condition warrants active treatment.

The precise reason why some people develop acne yet others do not is unknown. However, hormonal factors appear to set the stage for the development of the condition. Except for in the first few months of life, the disease does not develop before puberty, nor does it occur in eunuchs unless they are treated with male hormones. Acne is aggravated by the administration of male hormones, and of course premenstrual exacerbations are common in women. Without the natural oils secreted in the skin, known as sebum, there would be no acne. Without male hormones there is little if any sebum. Genetic factors, however, have a definite influence, as do bacteria, which are involved in the development of inflammation. Dietary and emotional factors are sometimes implicated, but their connection has not been completely proven.

Acne occurs at an age when the adolescent is adjusting, sometimes with difficulty, to a major physical and emotional transition. Teenagers are often self-conscious, and unduly embarrassed by even minor grades of the disease. To dismiss acne as unimportant demonstrates a considerable lack of understanding, particularly as the disease can be satisfactorily suppressed in the majority of patients, and scarring prevented or minimised.

There are three basic factors that set the stage for the development of acne. The first is excessive production of oil (sebum) by the oil glands, mainly situated on the face, chest and back. These sebaceous glands are controlled by male hormones present in both sexes.

The second is the tendency for the ducts leading from the glands to the skin's surface to become blocked. The stimulus for this is also thought to be hormonal, or due to excessive amounts of oil having to pass through the duct. This blockage is then known as a comedone, or 'blackhead'. The colour is not due to dirt but to melanin in the stratum corneum. Eventually, if the duct remains blocked and oil production continues, the gland will rupture.

The third factor, then, is the release of bacteria with the oil into the subcutaneous tissue, provoking an intense inflammatory reaction, known as a pimple or 'zit'.

There are four classical types of acne:

1. *Infantile*: This occurs in the first few months of life, affects boys mainly, and is resolved spontaneously.
2. *Adolescent*: This is the commonest type, which occurs around puberty and frequently needs treatment.
3. *Cosmetica*: This is associated with the prolonged or excessive use of cosmetics. In particular, we find that moisturisers, foundation cream, heavy make-up and regular facials are potent causative factors.
4. *Oil*: This occurs mainly on the legs of workers exposed to petroleum products.

Certain drugs may also precipitate or aggravate acne. These include:

- steroids
- phenytoin
- lithium
- iodides or bromides
- quinine
- chloral hydrate.

Acne can be a devastating disease, coming as it often does at a time when young people wish to look their best, and identify with the beautiful idols of their peer group. Many parents are heard to tell their children that they will 'grow out of it', that 'it will clear when you turn 21' or 'when you marry'; finally, if it has not improved as predicted it would, by the time that 'you have children', the sufferers often angrily seek active treatment.

Fortunately, most cases clear up with little or no help. However, the severity of the disorder will depend on a person's hormone balance and the receptivity of the oil glands. At about the time of adolescence, many hormonal and emotional changes are under way. We all possess endocrine glands (such as the adrenals, ovaries or testicles, and thyroid) that secrete hormones into the blood stream. These are chemicals that regulate the function of other endocrine glands as well as the blood vessels, oil glands, hair follicles and so forth. There is a close link between the endocrine and nervous systems which is controlled by a gland attached to the base of the brain called the pituitary. As a result of this link, emotional situations will affect a person's hormones. Consequently, as a result of, for example, premenstrual or examination stress, the skin tends to become oilier and 'break out'.

This interaction between a person's emotions and hormones is essential to the understanding and subsequent treatment of patients with acne. Many individuals have their social, emotional and even professional lives ruined because they do not have 'a clear skin'. Consequently it is most important for such people to seek sympathetic counselling and appropriate care. The condition may not seem too bad to an observer, but if it upsets an individual's self-esteem or body image, treatment is essential.

THE SEQUENCE OF EVENTS LEADING TO A PUSTULE

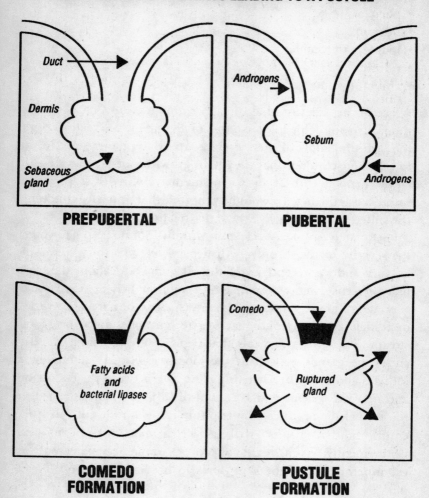

PREPUBERTAL

Duct

Dermis

Sebaceous gland

PUBERTAL

Androgens

Sebum

Androgens

COMEDO FORMATION

Fatty acids and bacterial lipases

PUSTULE FORMATION

Comedo

Ruptured gland

Treatment

It is important for acne sufferers to understand the pathology of the condition, in particular the role of hormones, comedones and bacteria. They should understand that acne is not an infectious or dietary disorder, and that it can be brought under control and scarring avoided. Looked at objectively, it will be seen that for successful treatment three criteria must be achieved:

1. unblocking of the ducts.
2. reduction of the bacteria in the oil.
3. reduction of the activity of the oil glands.

1. Unblocking of the follicular openings (pores)

There are various applications that may be applied to the skin which will help unblock the pores, destroy the blackheads and allow the oil to be discharged onto the skin's surface in the normal manner. Older preparations such as various drying lotions containing *salicylic acid* or *sulphur* are quite effective. *Benzoyl peroxide*, in varying strengths, is a newer and very effective agent. It has an antibacterial as well as unblocking effect. One should start with the weaker concentration and gradually build up to avoid skin irritation.

Retinoic acid (Tretinoin) is the newest exfoliant. It also comes in various strengths and bases. It acts by increasing the turnover rate of the epidermal cells in the duct, thereby reducing their cohesiveness. Consequently, old comedones disintegrate and fewer new ones form. Care should be taken with this preparation during the summer months as it may make the skin more prone to sunburn. This can be minimised if the preparation is used only at night and a light SPF 15 sunscreen worn during the day. It is also wise to commence treatment with the weaker gel before progressing to the stronger cream.

2. Reduction of the bacteria in the sebum (oil)

Antibiotics reduce the number of bacteria in the sebaceous glands. As a result, fewer enzymes, which are chemicals that break down the oil into irritant acids, are formed. Consequently, when the gland ruptures there is much less associated inflammation. Only very small doses of oral antibiotics are required to achieve this, much less than for normal skin infections. Therefore they may be used for prolonged periods, except of course during pregnancy, in children under the age of 12 years, or if side effects appear. Oral antibiotics are the most effective, particularly tetracyclines, which are soluble in sebum. Other effective antibiotics include doxycycline, erythromycin or minocycline.

Topical antibiotics, which are applied to the skin, may also be used, particularly during pregnancy or if the patient cannot tolerate oral antibiotics. Either erythromycin or clindamycin may be used, although they are not as effective as the oral form. In fact, some trials have shown that they are not as effective as benzoyl peroxide for treating mild acne.

3. Reduction of sebaceous gland activity

A significant reduction in the rate of sebum production results in a marked improvement in acne. The activity of the oil or sebaceous glands is male-hormone (androgen) dependent. Therefore, anything that reduces androgen will be helpful in this condition.

Hormonal therapy should be considered for females who do not respond to other treatment, and particularly those with premenstrual exacerbations of acne. *Oestrogen therapy* is the most effective, and the most convenient method of taking it is as the oral contraceptive pill. Oestrogen in a daily dose of fifty micrograms or more will reduce sebum production by 40 per cent after three months' treatment. Most oral contraceptives, particularly the 'mini-pills', have a predominantly androgenic effect and therefore may worsen acne. It is important to take a non-androgenic progestogen and moderate levels of oestrogen, such as in the sequential varieties.

Other anti-androgenic drugs also exist that, again, can only be used by females. *Spironolactone* is a diuretic with a strong anti-androgenic effect on the hair follicle and the sebaceous gland. Consequently, it is of value in both the treatment of excessive hair and acne. This drug blocks both androgen production and androgen reception at the sebaceous gland. It may cause irregular periods and masculinisation of a female foetus, so to prevent conception it is advisable for women to take oral contraceptives as well.

Cyproterone acetate is a similar but stronger anti-androgen. It also blocks androgen production and reception, and needs to be taken in conjunction with an oral contraceptive.

An important advance in the treatment of severe, cystic acne has come about with the development of retinoids. Drugs belonging to this group are not hormones but synthetic vitamin A derivatives. They are therefore particularly suitable for males.

Isotretinoin is the currently available retinoid for the treatment of cystic acne. Its mode of action includes marked reduction in the size of sebaceous glands, with an accompanying 75–90 per cent reduction in sebum production. It also has an effect on the lining of the sebaceous ducts, greatly decreasing their tendency to become blocked by comedones. Treatment usually takes four to six months, by which time the condition has usually been cured!

Some adverse reactions are common, particularly extreme dryness of the skin generally and the lips in particular. Dryness of the eyes may make wearing contact lenses uncomfortable, and dryness in the nose may cause nose bleeds. Cholesterol and triglyceride levels may rise temporarily, and the skin may be more susceptible to sunburn. All these reactions, however, disappear on completion of treatment, and I have never had a patient who felt that these reactions were sufficiently annoying to outweigh the advantages and therefore stop treatment. The most important side effect for women is the possibility of birth defects in their children. Appropriate contraception must be commenced one month prior to starting therapy and continued for at least three months after cessation.

Acne surgery
In spite of adequate treatment, some scarring may result and may take the form of quite large persistent cysts. These may be treated by drainage followed by injecting a steroid preparation into the cavity. This promotes shrinkage and healing.

Deep 'ice-pick' scars may either be excised and sutured or incised around the periphery and elevated to skin level.

More superficial 'undulating' scars respond well to collagen implants, which are injected under scars to lift them.

More severe or extensive scarring may require dermabrasion. This involves planing the skin to a smoother or more even contour using a rapidly rotating diamond-chip disc. The local anaesthetic spray used also freezes the skin to make it firm to work on. All these procedures may be performed in a dermatologist's office.

Acne is a common disorder of the oil gland system. Unfortunately it usually affects adolescents at a very critical time of life. If the condition is severe or chronic it warrants active treatment, the aim of which is to reduce inflammation, improve the appearance and minimise scarring. Sympathetic counselling and an appropriate selection of treatment options are most important for good results.

VARIANTS OF ACNE
There are two common variants of acne.

Perioral dermatitis
This is a very characteristic acne-like dermatitis of the lower face. It occurs exclusively in females, around the mouth and on the chin, sparing the skin just around the lips. The pimples are usually multiple, small, red and not usually pustular. Most frequently this condition appears during pregnancy or in women taking oral contraceptives. This may occur several years after commencing 'the pill', and is more common with the 'mini-pill'.

Treatment
The condition is frequently treated as a dermatitis with steroid creams, usually stronger fluorinated ones, which may initially improve the appearance but actually prolong the course of the condition.

Treatment with oral tetracyclines, and discontinuing topical steriods, usually cures the problem.

Rosacea
This is a common disorder of the facial skin characterised by diffuse redness and inflamed pustules. The condition mainly affects the middle-aged and elderly. Blind or pustular pimples usually appear on a background of redness and superficial blood vessels. Unlike acne, there are no blackheads or scarring. If severe, the skin of the nose may become thickened, very red and irregularly swollen. About one third of patients with rosacea suffer also from inflammation of the eyes. The disease is often chronic and aggravated by anything that causes the facial skin to become flushed.

Treatment

Treatment with tetracyclines is very effective, and only very small doses may be required on a long-term basis. Factors that promote facial flushing should also be avoided. These include excessive sun exposure, heat, alcohol, smoking and spicy food. The application of metronidazole gel is also helpful. Occasionally, plastic surgery may be necessary if enlargement of the nose becomes a problem.

AIDS

Human immunodeficiency virus (HIV) infection results in a spectrum of disease, with acquired immune deficiency syndrome (AIDS) as its end stage. Dermatologists were among the first to identify the sudden, unexplained rise in unusual infections and skin malignancies, in 1981, amongst homosexual men in New York and California. We are now a full decade into an epidemic that has rapidly spread throughout the world, causing a major health problem. The latest statistics (1991) from the USA indicate that over 160 000 cases have been reported since 1981, and that 100 000 people have died of AIDS. The World Health Organisation estimates that there are more than 300 000 AIDS cases, and about ten million people infected with the virus.

The HIV is thought to have originated in African monkeys. It is a so-called retrovirus, which means it is very slow-growing. Some Africans eat monkeys and drink their blood, and of course they may be bitten by monkeys. In this way the virus may have entered the human race. The virus destroys certain white blood cells known as T-lymphocytes, which are essential for the body's natural immune system that protects us against infections and other diseases.

The virus is usually transmitted sexually, or through blood and blood products. It is not transmitted by casual household contact such as sharing utensils, nor by personal contact such as kissing or hugging. The disease is most likely to affect homosexual men, intravenous drug abusers, recipients of HIV-contaminated blood or blood products, and haemophiliacs, as well as the sexual partners and children of HIV-infected persons.

People with HIV infection are prone to develop severe opportunistic infections and an unusual type of skin cancer. But a number of common skin conditions also frequently occur more severely and are more difficult to treat in HIV-infected people than in healthy individuals. The commonest life-threatening infection that patients with AIDS are prone to is a severe and unusual kind of lung infection called *pneumocystis carinii pneumonia*. It is due to a common parasite that does not cause infections in healthy individuals.

The most common skin manifestation of AIDS is *Kaposi's sarcoma*. Kaposi's sarcoma is a very rare form of skin cancer that develops in about 20 per cent of cases. It usually appears as one or more symptomless lumps on the skin or in the mouth. Their colour may vary from pink to dark red, purple or brown, and they may be mistaken for insect bites, birthmarks or bruises. They range in size from that of a pinhead to a large coin, and may continue to enlarge into thick lumps or growths. Occasionally Kaposi's sarcoma can involve lymph nodes and internal organs.

There are also a number of common skin conditions that may occur more frequently, or more severely, in association with HIV infection. Most of these diseases are also seen in healthy individuals and do not necessarily indicate HIV infection.

Skin infections are particularly common—especially viral ones. *Herpes simplex* infections usually appear around the mouth or nose, and are sometimes called 'fever blisters' or 'cold sores'. Repeated herpes infections also occur in the eyes and on the anal or genital regions, but any area of the skin may be involved. Before the blisters or ulcers develop, the involved area usually becomes red and is accompanied by burning, itching or pain. The clusters of tiny blisters break, leaving small ulcers that may crust over or develop scabs. The lesions usually heal within five to ten days. People infected with HIV tend to experience more frequent outbreaks and more severe ones with large, painful ulcerations that often increase in size and last for three to four weeks or longer.

Herpes zoster, also known as 'shingles', is due to reactivation of the chicken pox virus, which has lain dormant in the body since childhood. The eruption appears suddenly, in a band-like pattern, limited to an area of the skin on one side of the body. In the beginning the involved area becomes tender and red, and is accompanied by a deep throbbing pain. Clusters of multiple blisters appear which soon burst, leaving ulcers that then become scabs.

The severe pain typical of herpes zoster is due to inflammation of the infected nerves in the region involved. This painful condition can last for several weeks and may spread to other parts of the body, with blisters developing that look like chicken pox. The eruption of shingles, particularly in a younger person, may be the first sign of infection with HIV due to a weakened immune system.

Molluscum contagiosa are viral skin lesions commonly seen in children. They appear as smooth, pearly or waxy skin-coloured lumps that vary in size from that of a pin-head to a large pea. They have a central core filled with white cheesy material. They are neither painful nor itchy. Persons infected with HIV may suddenly develop large numbers of these lesions on almost any part of the skin.

Warts are caused by the papilloma virus. When they occur in HIV-infected individuals they usually occur in the genital and anal region and tend to be larger, more numerous, and widespread. They are also particularly resistant to standard, usually-effective forms of treatment.

'Hairy' leukoplakia of the mouth is an unusual condition characterised by small, white, fuzzy patches, most commonly on the tongue. It is believed to be caused by the Epstein-Barr virus, and has so far only been observed in HIV-infected individuals. 'Hairy' leukoplakia resembles, and can be confused with, 'thrush', a yeast infection of the mouth, also commonly seen in HIV-infected individuals.

Fungal infections involving various parts of the body, including the mouth, vagina, anus and the skin folds, are more prevalent in association with HIV infection. Usually they are caused by the yeast *Candida albicans*, also known as monilia or 'thrush'. When such infections develop in the mouth they are called *oral candidiasis*. It appears as white, curd-like patches on the tongue

143

and inner surfaces of the cheeks. These are easily scraped off. Unlike 'hairy' leukoplakia, it usually causes a soreness of the mouth or throat, difficulty in swallowing and loss of taste.

Both adults and infants who have HIV infection, and AIDS, frequently develop yeast infections characterised by a severe, itchy red rash involving the skin folds of the groin, often spreading onto the genitals and buttocks or thighs. Women who are immune-suppressed may develop severe vaginitis due to candidiasis, with a milky discharge and white patches on the vaginal lining. These infections occur frequently, repeatedly, and are very resistant to treatment in patients with HIV infection and AIDS.

Bacterial infections are also common in HIV-infected individuals. Intravenous drug abusers often develop abscesses at the injection site. However, more commonly we see *impetigo*, characterised by the widespread development of multiple clusters of large, soft, fluid-filled blisters that tend to break easily, oozing yellowish liquid. Once the blisters of impetigo break, large shallow ulcers remain, which become covered by a yellow crust. In immune-suppressed people, who frequently develop bacterial skin infections, there is a danger that the infections may spread to the bloodstream and then throughout the body. Consequently, intravenous antibiotic therapy is usually required.

Some *non-infectious skin diseases* are also much more common, more severe, and more difficult to treat, in HIV-infected people. These are described in other chapters, and include:

- seborrhoeic dermatitis
- psoriasis
- urticaria
- folliculitis/acne

As previously mentioned, most of these skin conditions are quite commonly seen in otherwise healthy individuals. However, if these conditions are particularly severe, recur frequently, are resistant to treatment, or are seen in someone who is at high risk of contracting the HIV, then one must consider immune-suppression, possibly related to an underlying infection with HIV.

ALLERGIES

Allergic reactions, in some form, occur in all individuals. This may be beneficial—as in the antibody response to infection or to protective vaccines. But reactions may also be harmful—as in a reaction to something taken internally or applied externally. Then there is a group of diseases that may affect the skin and also other organs, which are auto-allergic, known as auto-immune diseases.

DRUG REACTIONS

Allergic reactions to medication taken orally or injected are common. They have become more common with the increasing age and the increasing medication of the population.

Classically, the rash is of sudden onset and may be accompanied by a fever. It is normally symmetrical, blotchy, like measles or hives, and mainly affects the trunk. It usually clears within one or two weeks of stopping the drug, but will recur if the drug is taken again. A drug allergy can develop suddenly, even after several years of trouble-free medication, and there is probably no drug that never causes a reaction.

Even intelligent individuals are surprisingly vague about what medication they take. Frequently they forget that they are taking vitamins, purgatives, analgesics, or the birth-control pill.

Measles-like rashes are generally caused by:

• penicillin
• sulphonamides
• barbiturates
• allopurinol
• non-steroidal anti-inflammatories.

Hive-like rashes are generally caused by:

• salicylates
• penicillin
• insulin
• quinine
• vaccines.

145

Many other patterns of reaction may occur. Careful detective work may be necessary to sort out which drug is involved. Sometimes all drugs may have to be stopped and gradually re-introduced before any conclusion can be drawn. Unfortunately, there is still no reliable skin or blood test for the diagnosis of such a drug reaction.

CONTACT DERMATITIS

This is a form of eczema that may develop as a reaction of the skin to contact with a foreign substance. Contact dermatitis is probably the commonest skin disease in industrialised countries. It seems that the higher the degree of industrialisation, the higher the incidence of this problem. In fact, occupational contact dermatitis accounts for nearly 50 per cent of all occupational illnesses in the USA and 90 per cent of US workers' compensation claims.

There are two forms of this reaction. The first is *allergic contact dermatitis*, which is the result of a true allergic reaction to the substance contacted. The second form is *irritant contact dermatitis*, which is not an allergic reaction but the result of damage caused by direct chemical action.

Allergic contact dermatitis

This often occurs in response to a substance previously handled frequently and without ill effect. But once established, this allergy may persist for months, years, or a lifetime. The diagnosis can usually be made by a detailed description of what happened and how; by the appearance of the rash; and particularly the location of the rash. Patch Tests may be required in difficult cases, to either make or confirm the diagnosis. These tests involve the application to the patient's unaffected skin of various substances suspected of having caused the problem. Mostly, these more-frequent possible allergens are pre-packaged in sealed foil strips that are opened and applied to the back. Sometimes 'one-off', special Patch Tests may be made using a small square of gauze, impregnated with the substance. The patch is then covered with an impermeable dressing. The tests are left on for twenty-four to forty-eight hours before being removed by the patient. His or her back is then examined

ALLERGY ATLAS

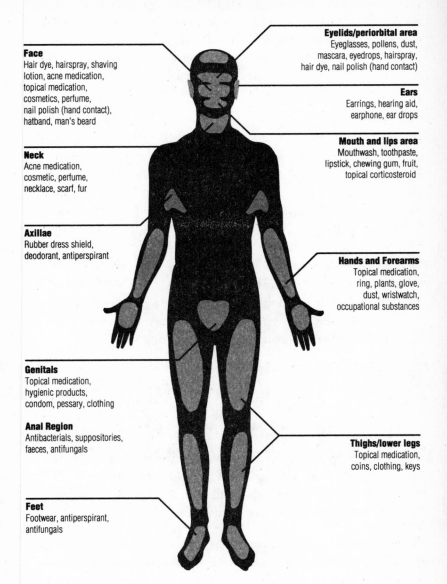

Eyelids/periorbital area
Eyeglasses, pollens, dust,
mascara, eyedrops, hairspray,
hair dye, nail polish (hand contact)

Face
Hair dye, hairspray, shaving
lotion, acne medication,
topical medication,
cosmetics, perfume,
nail polish (hand contact),
hatband, man's beard

Ears
Earrings, hearing aid,
earphone, ear drops

Mouth and lips area
Mouthwash, toothpaste,
lipstick, chewing gum, fruit,
topical corticosteroid

Neck
Acne medication,
cosmetic, perfume,
necklace, scarf, fur

Axillae
Rubber dress shield,
deodorant, antiperspirant

Hands and Forearms
Topical medication,
ring, plants, glove,
dust, wristwatch,
occupational substances

Genitals
Topical medication,
hygienic products,
condom, pessary, clothing

Anal Region
Antibacterials, suppositories,
faeces, antifungals

Thighs/lower legs
Topical medication,
coins, clothing, keys

Feet
Footwear, antiperspirant,
antifungals

by the dermatologist twenty-four to forty-eight hours later. A positive allergic reaction appears like a bad mosquito bite within twenty-four hours, and persists. A positive irritant reaction appears quickly, is flat and red, and fades rapidly.

The most common causes of allergic contact dermatitis are: plants, metal, clothing, rubber, cosmetics, medication and occupational substances.

Plants frequently involved are:
• Rhus tree
• poison ivy
• compositae in the Australian bush
• chrysanthemums
• callistemon ('bottle-brush')
• Primula *obconica*.

Metals frequently involved are:
• nickel—jewellery, watch-bands, jeans studs, brassiere hooks.
• chromium—cement, paints, anti-corrosive agents, photographic and offset printing material.
• cobalt—jewellery, clothing, plastics, printing ink.

Clothing. Reaction is mainly due to:
• resins—added to fibres to make them drip-dry or crease resistant.
• dyes—to colour fabrics.
• leather tanning agents—mainly in footwear.

Rubber. Rubber allergy is common and is usually due to either the accelerators or anti-oxidants used in manufacture. It is frequently found in footwear, waistbands, or other elasticised areas, and of course rubber gloves or condoms.

Cosmetics. Nail cosmetics that cause these reactions are either the resin in the nail enamel, the acrylic monomer in artificial nails, or formaldehyde in nail hardeners.

Lipstick problems may arise from the colouring agent, the perfume, or lanolin. Hair preparations that may be suspect include dyes, sprays, or shampoos.

Medicaments most commonly involved are:
- local anaesthetics
- antibiotics
- antiseptics
- anti-histamines
- lanolin
- preservatives.

Occupational substances most commonly involved include:
- chromium—in cement or paints.
- nickel—in nickel plating or the metal itself.
- plants and plant products, such as flowers, sawdust, vegetables or turpentine.
- many chemicals, drugs, organic dyes, rubber additives.
- uncured plastics, such as epoxyresins or acrylic plastics.

Irritant contact dermatitis

This can be produced in any individual, provided the chemical irritant is applied in a strong enough concentration, and for a sufficient length of time. It is *not* an allergic reaction. The irritants may be classified as strong or weak.

Strong irritants injure the skin on first contact, producing severe inflammation, for example, strong acids or alkalis.

Weak irritants require repeated or prolonged contact to cause inflammation, for example, detergents, and excessive exposure to water. Primary irritant eczema of this kind is caused and perpetuated by a variety of factors, some of which may break down the barrier properties of the skin, while others inflict damage on the vulnerable skin once this has happened.

The areas most likely to be affected are those most exposed to daily irritation—the hands and forearms. The commonest form of the condition is seen in housewives' hands, and is called 'housewives' dermatitis' (or 'dishpan hands'). It is suffered by about 1 per cent of women, particularly mothers with young children. The winter months, when the temperature is lower and the circulation poorer, are the worst for this condition. Humidity is also lower in the winter, allowing the skin to dry, lose its elasticity and crack. Repeated wetting and drying alters the natural defences of the outermost layers of the skin, so that substances commonly encountered in household work penetrate the skin more easily and cause irritation. These include household soaps, detergents, foods (particularly citrus fruit, potatoes and tomatoes), household chemicals, polishes and soil. Of course any pre-existing skin problem or abrasion, as well as bacteria or fungal infections, may also play a role. In addition, 40–50 per cent of women with housewives' dermatitis will show a positive patch test to at least one of a battery of common allergens.

Although the setting in which irritant contact dermatitis occurs is complex, people can do many things to prevent or minimise the problem. These include washing hands as seldom as possible and, if wet work is unavoidable, wearing cotton gloves under rubber ones, or plastic gloves with cotton lining. Tasks that require the wearing of gloves include such things as cutting up meat and vegetables, peeling fruit and potatoes, bathing the baby, and shampooing hair. Whenever the sufferer's hands are wet, they must be well dried, and a good hand-cream immediately applied each and every time. Special attention should be given to the area of skin under a person's rings, as this is a common and persistent source of trouble, not from allergy to the rings but from trapped noxious substances. Irritant dermatitis is also seen on children's feet, particularly in winter, and may be aggravated by the cold or by wearing nylon socks and rubber footwear.

Primary irritant hand eczema is also seen in manual workers, particularly those who work with oils or some of the many chemicals that are now used in industry. One of the more important aspects of industrial medicine is the provision of adequate protection for workers from the harmful effects of such substances.

No test has been devised to confirm the diagnosis of irritant contact dermatitis, since patch testing will produce a positive reaction in most people if the concentration and duration of application is appropriate. Diagnosis is made on a knowledge of the irritant potential of the substances contacted, on the patient's history and on the clinical appearance of the disorder.

The most common causes of irritant contact dermatitis are:

- soaps, detergents, solvents and water
- fibreglass
- resinous plastics
- petroleum oils, greases and fuels
- cutting oils and coolants
- agricultural chemicals.

AUTO-IMMUNITY

Here the word 'immunity' does not mean protection from, but rather a reaction against, something: in this case, auto—which is derived from the Greek 'autos', or self. In other words, this is an allergic reaction to normal body tissues.

The body has appropriate mechanisms to prevent the recognition of 'self' tissue as antigens by the lymphoid system but, as with all machinery, there is always the possibility of a breakdown. In fact, the older the individual, the greater the chance of malfunction. When this happens 'auto-antibodies'—antibodies that react against 'self' tissues—are produced. These auto-immune disorders form a spectrum. At one end are *organ-specific diseases,* with organ-specific auto-antibodies, for example pemphigus; and at the other end, *non-organ-specific diseases,* for example systemic lupus erythematosus. SLE affects the skin, kidneys, joints, blood vessels, and so on, whereas pemphigus has specific auto-antibodies against the epidermis and these can be demonstrated both in the skin and the serum of patients with this disease. Because of this allergic reaction to the epidermis itself, very large blisters form both on the skin and the linings of the mouth, eyes or genitals. Although rare, it is a potentially fatal skin disease.

ECZEMA

Eczema and dermatitis are often regarded as synonymous. Dermatitis, however, simply means inflammation of the skin, of which there are various forms. By contrast, eczema is a distinctive pattern of inflammatory response with distinctive microscopic changes, and internal rather than external associations.

151

The word 'eczema' comes from the Greek *ekzeo*, to boil over. In an acute case of eczema, the skin becomes red and swollen, and its surface oozes and/or blisters, which results in crusting and scaling. The chronic cases end up with thickened skin, evidence of scratch marks, and increased pigmentation.

In infancy, the most common but by no means the only form of eczema is *atopic eczema*. The term 'atopic' indicates an inherited tendency to develop one or more of a related group of common conditions, such as asthma, hay fever, urticaria or eczema. It is estimated that 10 per cent of the population are atopics, and that hay fever is the most common manifestation. Eczema affects about 3 per cent of infants, and these have a one in four chance of developing asthma or hay fever some time later.

Atopic eczema (AE) usually appears in the infant between the ages of 3 months and 2 years. The initial site of inflammation is commonly the face and scalp, with subsequent spreading to the limbs. The condition is worst during infancy, and becomes milder and more localised by puberty. Many sufferers have a complete remission by about 6 years of age, and by puberty at least half of those affected are free of the disease. The remainder are clear by about 30 years of age.

There are various theories about what causes atopic eczema, but the only certainty is that many factors are responsible for the condition.

The first factors are immunological ones. People with AE have greatly increased immuno-globulin E antibodies (IgE) in their blood. Consequently they are abnormally sensitive to common, and usually harmless, antigens. This also means that with a prick test on the skin or radio-allergo-sorbent tests (RAST) on the blood, they will react against a wide variety of antigens, including foods, pollens, moulds and insects. Unfortunately, though, because of their hypersensitivity, there is a very poor correlation between positive RAST or prick tests to a particular allergen and aggravation of the eczema following the actual exposure to it.

The role of food allergy in AE is controversial. In fact in the majority of people, estimated at about 90 per cent, food allergy plays no part whatsoever. Careful elimination of suspected allergens, followed by re-challenging, are the only satisfactory ways of identifying possible food allergens.

About 80 per cent of people with AE have some degree of defective white cell function (T lymphocytes) in the blood, resulting in impaired cell-mediated immunity. The increased susceptibility of these people to viral infections is a manifestation of this abnormality.

The second important factor is the inherent irritability of the skin. This means that these individuals have a lowered itch threshold. Consequently, stimuli that on normal skin would simply produce a touch sensation are interpreted as an itch. Itch then leads to scratch, which further aggravates the eczema.

The third factor is the abnormal blood vessel response of the skin. Following light touch or scratching of the skin, instead of the blood vessels dilating and producing a red mark, they constrict, leaving a white mark. This is due to an imbalance in the activity of the autonomic nervous system, which might also explain the intense irritability of the skin.

The fourth factor relates to the skin's abnormal dryness. This appears to be due to an abnormal stratum corneum that lacks sufficient lipids to hold water. This is probably due to impaired oil gland function, resulting in a dry and therefore itchy skin.

Many infants with atopic eczema also suffer with a 'fish-scale' condition known as *ichthyosis*. Accompanying this there is also an impaired sweat gland function. This results in a poor response to temperature or climatic changes and an increased tendency to overheat. This also results in a more itchy skin.

Finally, people with AE are very prone to develop skin infections. This is due to fine cracks in the dry, brittle skin that allow the entry of bacterial, viral or fungal organisms. The impaired cell immunity in the skin, that allows infection to take hold more easily, is also a contributing factor. Consequently, infection is commonly the sole cause of aggravation of AE.

Various factors are known to trigger an attack of eczema. These include external irritants, climatic changes and psychological factors. Stress may induce itching, and scratching will cause the eczema. The type of eczema that develops varies from individual to individual. Rather than the classical *flexural eczema* in the creases of the skin, some people develop coin-like spots, mainly over the limbs, known as *discoid eczema*. Alternately, the eczema may simply affect the fingers or toes, with small water-filled blisters forming underneath the skin, known as *dyshidrotic eczema*. Some cases, however, only show white, rounded patches, mainly over the shoulders or on the cheeks, and this is known as *pityriasis alba*. Others may simply exhibit rather dry, irritable skin, without any redness or oozing, known as *asteatotic eczema*.

Treatment

The treatment of any condition, particularly eczema, is related to correction or modification of the abnormalities causing the problem. Since children with atopic eczema have impaired oil gland function, resulting in a dry skin, the first important step is to counteract this. This means infrequent bathing or showering, with the temperature of the water kept cool and a minimum of soap used. Bath oil may be very useful, as are soap substitutes such as emulsifying ointment. Simple moisturisers should be applied whenever necessary, and particularly after bathing, to help trap the moisture in the skin. Petroleum jelly (Vaseline) is cheap and effective, but preparations such as 5 per cent glycerin in aqueous cream may be equally useful. Urea-containing preparations should be avoided as the urea frequently irritates sensitive skin. Similarly, perfumed products, or those containing antiseptics, even bubble baths, should be avoided. The condition of these children will be worse during the winter when humidity is lower, and this may be aggravated by central heating that is associated with less humidity in the rooms. Humidifiers can be very helpful in these cases.

Due to impaired sweat gland function, it is advisable to keep these children cool rather than allowing them to become overheated, and to avoid rapid temperature changes, since their skin will not adequately cope with these, and will become itchy. Due to the children's lower itch threshold, it is advisable for them to avoid irritants such as wool or synthetics next to the skin, as these may stimulate itching. Similarly, it is worthwhile considering cuffs on pyjamas or mittens to restrain such children from subconsciously scratching while they are asleep, further damaging their already easily-irritated skin.

Expensive *skin testing* with regard to various potential allergens is quite useless for these individuals. Because of their extremely sensitive skin, due to their increased IgE levels, they will exhibit positive reactions to most substances with which they are tested. Such tests, then, have absolutely no bearing on their eczema. This type of testing may be useful in discovering a cause for asthma or hay fever, but not for eczema. Interestingly, these children are certainly more prone to irritant types of contact dermatitis, but no more prone than normal individuals to a true allergic contact dermatitis.

The overall management of atopic eczema requires time to explain the disease to the parents, time to discuss the particular case and the various factors involved in treatment. This requires patience on the part of the doctor as well as the family. In particular, the treatment may involve manipulation of the environment, the application of creams to the skin, the taking of various oral medications and, to a very limited extent, 'allergic' treatment or psychotherapy. The condition does not have one single cause, nor one single magical cure. However, it can be most adequately controlled with the cooperation (and this includes the active participation) of the patient and family.

Specific applications that will reduce itching and aid the healing of the skin include various bland emollients such as aqueous cream or emulsifying ointment, and numerous tar-based creams or ointments, which have a similar effect to some cortisone preparations. Corticosteroid preparations have an anti-inflammatory action, allowing inflamed or damaged skin to heal. They also have an immuno-suppressive action, thereby diminishing local antibody production. It is important to remember that, where possible, the less strong cortisone preparations, such as hydrocortisone cream, should be used in preference to the stronger fluorinated creams such as Betnovate, Synalar, and so on.

Ultraviolet light, particularly UVB, can be very useful in some cases. This, of course, includes sunlight, which has an immuno-suppressant effect on the skin. This is one reason why AE frequently improves during the summer months. The other reason is the increased humidity or moisture content of the air.

Oral medication such as various anti-histamines tends to reduce the intensity of the itch and lessen the tendency to scratch. It also may have a sedative effect, and so be useful at night to help the child sleep better, scratch less, and consequently damage the skin less. Oral cortisone should always be avoided unless absolutely essential.

Eczema frequently becomes infected, and in such cases oral antibiotics may be very useful. In general, it is better to treat infection with oral antibiotics than with antibiotic creams. More potent cortisone-based creams are of course sometimes necessary, but they should be reserved for sparing and infrequent use on the more severely-affected areas of the skin. This is because of their well-known local and internal side effects, which are discussed elsewhere.

The place of *diet* in the management of these children is still not certain. Some workers have found that breastfeeding for as long as possible may delay the onset of atopic eczema in some predisposed children. This work has as yet not been confirmed. Some children improve when goats' milk or soya-based milk is substituted for cows' milk. This is usually only of benefit to children who show other evidence of milk-protein allergy, and rarely has any prolonged benefit for children with eczema alone. The poor correlation between positive prick and RAST tests and subsequent food challenges should be remembered, and elimination diets not based on the results of these. Sometimes it is worth trying a simple diet, avoiding foods that are most likely to aggravate AE, such as cows' milk, eggs, beef, chicken, nuts and wheat. Six weeks is long enough to assess whether a diet is beneficial. However, most studies do not show complete clearance of the condition even with allergen avoidance. Occasionally, parents will notice that their child's ingestion of one or two specific foods is followed by severe itching, and it seems sensible for them then to avoid these foods. The withdrawal of potentially essential nutrients, in the hope that a cure for eczema might be found, is ill advised.

The *hospitalisation* of those cases of severe generalised eczema that do not respond to normal treatment is often extremely beneficial. This enables one to remove the child from a potential area of stress, and allows more adequate reassessment and the introduction of a controlled, supervised treatment program. In particular, it is very useful to be able to bandage the child adequately, so that skin that has been scratched has an opportunity to heal and regain its normal function. This can only be done by skilled nursing staff, who can then train the parents to follow this regimen at home if necessary. In hospital surroundings 'messy' creams and potions (which are often very useful) may be used without the parents becoming too upset about the appearance of their child's bed linen. In hospital it is also much easier to reintroduce a normal diet for children who have been unnecessarily restricted in this regard. It is a common experience for parents who may never have seen their child's skin normal and clear to be astounded, after one week's hospitalisation, at the sight of their child with normal skin—astounded at how the skin 'really looks'. Of course once the skin is back to normal it is much easier to keep it that way, and the parents should now have the confidence and skills required to do so.

What future or prognosis do these children have? It is often stated, quite correctly I believe, that children usually 'grow out of' eczema. This is because their oil and sweat glands mature and begin to function normally. Consequently, their skin becomes less dry, less easily overheated and irritable; so the attacks of eczema become less and less frequent. More specifically, however, the prognosis is related to whether the genetic predisposition is present in one or both parents.

The older child or adult with persistent eczema may have it localised to just the hands, the creases, or some other less important area. This group must avoid contact with sufferers of active cold sores, and should not receive smallpox vaccinations, as complications of a severe kind may result. These people would be best advised to avoid those occupations that involve contact with irritant chemicals, including oils, degreasing agents, and various hairdressing solutions. Other than this, it is important that affected children lead a normal life.

It must be stressed that children with eczema require continuing support and careful explanation of how they can learn to live within their skin's capabilities. They need reassurance that their life can be made more comfortable, and that no permanent disfigurement will result. Worrying, especially about such things as these, will lower the individual's threshold to skin irritation, and lead to more scratching and aggravation of the eczema.

Although the family must give a child with eczema special attention, it is important that the child not be allowed to 'rule the roost'; rather, firmness, with love, should be employed by the parents. When the child is older he or she must become an active participant in life rather than a passive recipient of treatment.

HAIR DISORDERS

Both hair and nails are derived from the epidermis, and both consist of the same dead tissue—the protein, keratin. Because of their derivation from the epidermis it is not surprising that diseases affecting the skin may affect the hair and nails as well. In addition, there are a number of disorders that are peculiar to the hair (including the scalp). The most common of these are discussed in this section.

DANDRUFF

This is a very common condition of the scalp for which treatment is sought. It is not, however, a disease. It is simply a physiological state that has been elevated to the status of a 'disease' solely on cosmetic grounds. About 50 per cent of the population suffer from it at some stage. Basically, dandruff consists of normal, dead skin cells that have been shed only to become trapped among the hairs of the scalp or in the oily sebum film. It is most common after puberty, and is absent on the bald scalp. Dandruff is not an infection, nor has it any relationship to hair loss. From the plethora of proprietary preparations sold over the counter it is obvious that dandruff concerns people, and that no one preparation suits all sufferers.

Treatment

Usually, dandruff may be satisfactorily controlled by the use of shampoos containing tar, selenium disulphide, or zinc pyrithione, all of which act by reducing the rate of normal skin shedding (turnover rate). Newer preparations include pirectone olanine and ketoconazole shampoo. Sometimes salicylic acid or corticosteroid creams are required intermittently to control the condition. If dandruff persists, or is severe, then you should consult a doctor, since you may be suffering with seborrhoeic dermatitis, eczema, or even psoriasis.

SEBORRHOEIC DERMATITIS

This condition is common and is a chronic inflammation of those skin areas having the greatest number of sebaceous (oil) glands. The affected skin is not only oily but inflamed, and covered with white or yellowish scales. It is often also itchy. Common sites for seborrhoeic dermatitis are the scalp, forehead, mid-face, eyebrows, ears and, in men, the chest. It is often associated with dandruff and 'cradle cap', but not always. The cause of the condition is not known, although it is a disease of adulthood. For some reason, not known, people who suffer with Parkinson's disease, or HIV infection, are often affected.

Treatment

This condition tends to come and go even without treatment. Unfortunately, it cannot be prevented, although it is not usually difficult to control. Once again, either a tar or zinc pyrithione shampoo may be beneficial. Sometimes specially prescribed salicylic acid and sulphur preparations, or cortisone preparations, are necessary for adequate treatment.

Cradle cap is a similar condition, and should be treated as for seborrhoeic dermatitis.

HAIR LOSS

Loss of hair may be temporary, when it is usually called *alopecia*; or it may be permanent—usually termed *baldness*.

Alopecia

The most common form of temporary diffuse alopecia is that associated with the following conditions or circumstances:

- acute mental stress
- severe illness or injury
- following pregnancy
- stopping the oral contraceptive pill
- iron deficiency
- various hormonal deficiencies
- certain drugs
- rapid weight loss.

In these cases the hairs in the resting phase are usually the ones lost. As such, the hair loss is temporary, and will right itself once the precipitating cause has been corrected.

Alopecia areata, where the loss is localised to one or more well-defined areas, is the most common type of hair loss seen in medical practice. There is sometimes a family history of it, and there appears to be a genetic association with some other conditions (known as auto-immune diseases) such as vitiligo (pigment loss), pernicious anaemia, and either over- or under-active thyroid disorders. Often psychological stress or some emotional deprivation was experienced some weeks prior to onset. Although alopecia areata occurs at all ages the majority of cases are in children and young adults. It is estimated that there are about 100 000 sufferers in Australia.

With this disorder patches of hair may be lost from any part of the body, although hair loss is typically limited to the scalp and beard areas. Symptomless bald areas up to a few centimetres in diameter develop, which may coalesce and produce the loss of all scalp hair (*alopecia totalis*) or even of the whole body (*alopecia universalis*). In the stage of active hair loss, very short, broken hairs shaped like exclamation marks may be found. These are not seen in the conditions which may, otherwise, be taken for alopecia areata (such conditions as ringworm and secondary syphilis).

Treatment

The prognosis for alopecia areata is good in the majority of cases, with most patients growing new, often initially white, hair within six to nine months. The longer the alopecia lasts and the larger the areas affected, the worse are the chances of satisfactory regrowth.

Small areas of hair loss that show evidence of regrowth are best left untreated. When improvement is slow or where areas are large, topical corticosteroids may be useful. Occasionally, they may be injected into the affected areas to promote regrowth, but this effect may be transient. Various irritants and sensitisers—such as DNCB—have been used in an attempt to stimulate hair growth, and more recently, minoxidil solution has been used. It is important for patients or parents to fully understand what is known about this condition and its varied course. Considerable reassurance is frequently necessary, and recently a number of self-help groups have been set up to enable those involved to help one another and to seek further help both from the government and the medical profession.

Baldness

Baldness in males is not a disease but an inherited predisposition. It is not confined to humans but also occurs in such other primates as chimpanzees and orang-outangs. After puberty all males undergo some change in the hair line and suffer some hair loss. The straight hair line on the forehead is replaced, after puberty, by a degree of recession on either side of the brow. Whether this will continue to extend, and will later be accompanied by thinning on the crown, depends on three factors. The two most important are whether or not there is a genetic background of baldness in the family, and whether normal male hormones are present. If, for example, a predisposed individual is castrated before puberty, he will not become bald. Should male hormones later be administered, he will become bald. Finally, there is the factor of age. By the age of 50, about 50 per cent of men have some degree

161

of baldness. Women are usually protected from baldness of this kind by their female hormones. After menopause, however, their hormone levels drop off and gradually baldness may develop. Occasionally hormone disorders may occur, causing both baldness of the scalp and excessive hair growth in other areas.

The onset of baldness in males is accompanied by shrinkage in the size of hair follicles. This results in the loosening of terminal hairs, which then gradually fall out and are replaced by immature vellus hairs. Ultimately these may also disappear, leaving scar tissue to replace the follicles. The rate of hair loss is very variable. Progression may be rapid or slow. Frequently, there is a rapid onset which then stabilises, with no further extension occurring for many years. Thinning and recession usually occurs in waves, interspersed with periods where there is no progression. If the individual is obtaining treatment during this stable period, he will ascribe the arrest of the hair loss to it: whereas actually, the arrest is the normal pattern for that individual, a pattern that cannot be influenced.

Treatment

There is no known treatment to either arrest the balding process or cause hair to regrow. Those cases where hair has been shown to appear on a previously bald scalp are cases of alopecia areata, where hair frequently returns anyhow. After adequate examination and careful, truthful explanation, philosophical acceptance may be the best advice that can be offered. If, however, active treatment is sought, various alternatives may be considered.

The latest medical approach has been the use of Minoxidil lotion. This drug was originally marketed to treat high blood pressure. Unfortunately it had many side effects, one of which was the development of excessive body hair. However, when used on the scalp only it has minimal, if any, side effects, but may, in some cases, cause hair to regrow. Minoxidil does not grow new hair, but appears to stimulate existing follicles to become more active. It must be applied twice daily for at least six months, and only 20 per cent of people obtain a reasonably satisfactory result. Unfortunately, treatment must continue indefinitely, otherwise the new hair disappears within a few months. Treatment is expensive, does not help everyone, and is a lifetime commitment.

There are also several surgical options. The first is a *hair transplant*. Here, small plugs or circles of hair-bearing scalp are removed from sites unlikely to go bald, such as the back and sides of the head. These are then replanted in appropriate spots on the bald scalp. Originally, each punch graft transplanted about fifteen hairs, which meant that the new hairs looked a bit like a toothbrush. Now, however, the technique is much more sophisticated and many grafts of three to five hairs may be used, or even micrografts of one hair, giving a more natural appearance. The second option is a *flap rotation*. Here, a strip of hair-bearing scalp is cut from the side of the head, left attached at one end with its blood supply, and rotated around to form a new hair line. The edges of the area that it was lifted from are then sewn together. The third option is a *scalp reduction*. Here, tissue expanders are placed under the bald scalp and slowly filled with saline to gradually stretch the skin. They are then removed and the loose skin cut away. The hair-bearing areas of skin at the sides of the scalp are then approximated in the middle and sewn together. The hair line can then be created with either a flap rotation or punch grafts. This method, although complicated, is very useful for the treatment of extensive baldness.

Artificial hair implantation is another method which I, however, strongly discourage. It consists of single synthetic fibres being implanted into the scalp using a fine needle. Each 'fibre' has a loop at the end around which tissue grows—because of the irritation it causes, thus holding the 'hair' in place. The problem with this method is that an allergic reaction to the artificial fibre is usually set up in the scar, resulting in inflammation, infection and frequently scarring around the fibre. Also, approximately 25 per cent of the 'hairs' will drop out within a year.

Hair fusion involves the attachment of a hairpiece to your own hair. Your hair is pulled through the mesh on the undersurface of the hairpiece, which is also held in place with clips, glue or double-sided tape. A major problem with this method is that, because the hairpiece is attached to your own hair, it starts to lift as the hair grows and so must be 're-fused' every month or so.

The hairpiece may also need to be replaced every year because hairs begin to fall out and the colour is generally bleached by the sun. Washing of the scalp is also extremely difficult, so hygiene may leave much to be desired.

Finally, there is the traditional standby of a wig or hairpiece, which is really a partial wig. These can appear very natural, depending on their quality. Some use real hair and are very well made and matched, and so are an excellent alternative to some of the methods discussed.

As I have said in an earlier chapter, the claims made for skin-care products bear little or no relation to their actual effect. When it comes to misleading the public, however, the cosmetic manufacturers pale in comparison with those involved in the business of 'treating' hair disorders. It is so lucrative a business that they do not hesitate to risk prosecution. A fine is a drop in the ocean compared with their profits, and if forced to close down they merely open up again under another name. Legally there is nothing to prevent anyone at all from setting up a 'hair clinic' or becoming a 'hair specialist' or 'trichologist'.

Whatever their title, the methods of hair clinics are always similar. A few hairs are taken from the client's scalp and examined by the practitioner, who wears a white coat. Scientific apparatus and coloured lights are usually evident in front of the client. These play an important part in setting the scene. A form is then filled out, making it all respectable; and lastly, of course, a diagnosis is made, the aim being to induce the client to embark on a course of 'treatment', the results of which are 'guaranteed'. As a rule, these courses involve a series of about twelve 'treatments' costing several hundred dollars (payable in advance) plus various products that are sold to the client to be used at home. The tragedy is that we have allowed the public to remain so misinformed that they accept the claims made by these people. This is also partly due to the fact that the most common scalp problems have no satisfactory medical cure.

The sporadic successes achieved by these businesses have two simple explanations: first, hair growth is cyclical, and periodically large amounts may be lost, frequently to be replaced again; second, spontaneous natural resolution is common for many scalp and hair disorders. Hair loss is not caused by excessive oil, dandruff, or poor circulation. Treating these conditions will not arrest, or reverse, baldness. Hair cannot be restored, or the loss slowed, by the application of any nutrient or tonic, nor by massage or electrical-laser stimulation. Some people will always exploit basic human desires, and the desire to appear attractive to others is especially vulnerable to exploitation. Hair, unfortunately, has lost most of its biological functions and has assumed a significant aesthetic and sexual role. The psychological importance of hair is often not fully appreciated until the hair is either lost or occurs in excess.

HIRSUTISM

Increased growth of facial and body hair is a common complaint amongst women attending endocrinology, gynaecology and dermatology clinics. The presence of fine vellus fuzz on the upper lip and chin is very common in women of all races. After the menopause this vellus hair is frequently accentuated by darker terminal hairs, which may appear interspersed among the finer hairs. There is considerable racial variation as regards hirsutism, with women of southern or eastern European extraction being more prone to excess hair, and women of Asian extraction—particularly the Japanese—being rarely affected. Often there is also a familial tendency to hirsutism.

When women are affected in those areas of the body which normally only develop hair in males, and particularly if this is associated with menstrual abnormalities, deepening of the voice, and frontal scalp recession, then there is most likely to be a correctable hormonal cause for the problem. Hormonal factors causing excessive hair growth include excessive male hormone production from either the adrenal glands, the pituitary gland, or certain rare ovarian tumours. Occasionally some drugs may be implicated—for example, dilantin, streptomycin, penicillamine, diazoxide, psoralens, and corticosteroids. Most women, however, show no clinical evidence of an endocrine disease or hormone abnormality, and this finding can of course be confirmed by appropriate blood and urine tests. If there is any doubt, these tests should be performed after medical assessment has been sought. In those cases of hirsutism where no abnormalities are suggested or found, the cause is probably excessive sensitivity of the hair follicles to the normal quantities of male hormones within the skin itself. Stress is also thought to be able to cause excess hair production by stimulating the over-production of male hormones via the pituitary gland, which has a close relationship with the brain.

Excess hair, particularly facial, has always been thought of as an undesirable characteristic in women. In men, for some reason, it is thought to denote virility. Witches are frequently illustrated with hair on the nose or chin. Graffiti often shows girls with moustaches, and so forth. Consequently many women find it upsetting to be hirsute. This commonly results in such feelings as irritability, frigidity, masculine trends, and impaired sexuality. As a result, treatment is frequently sought. Here again, we have a situation likely to be exploited: these unfortunate women are very susceptible to the promises of complete and permanent hair removal. From the number of establishments advertising the myth of permanent hair removal, one can get some idea of how many women must be seeking the hairless face. The actual incidence of hirsutism is impossible to assess. However, a survey of women students in Wales, in which the women were actually examined and questioned, showed that over one quarter had terminal hair on the face, and that in about 5 per cent of cases it was considered disfiguring.

Treatment

Obviously, if a major endocrine or hormonal disorder has been found, this may be corrected, possibly by surgery. If drugs are thought to be responsible, then on cessation of drug-taking the hair will disappear. Some minor hormonal causes may be treatable with a new male hormone antagonist called cyproterone acetate, or with a combination of dexamethasone to suppress the adrenals, and oestrogens to suppress the ovaries.

Failing this (that is, in about 95 per cent of cases) various physical procedures can be tried. Mild cases can be satisfactorily masked by simply bleaching dark hair with hydrogen peroxide. Depilatory creams, usually containing thioglycolates, are also reasonably effective in dissolving hair. Various cosmetic waxes, that are applied warm as a liquid and then allowed to harden before being peeled off, may be used to remove the hair that has stuck to the wax. Although this method is somewhat painful, it has the advantage that because the hair is removed at a lower level, it regrows more slowly, and with a naturally pointed tip; hence the bristly feel of hair cut at an angle by shaving is avoided.

Shaving is very effective but is strongly resisted by most women, often because of the rough feel of emerging hair and the masculine association. The belief that these procedures may encourage more rapid, coarser, or darker regrowth of hair must be strongly refuted. There is absolutely no evidence, in spite of careful investigation, to confirm this mistaken belief. The electronic tweezer, which holds the hair whilst a small electric current is applied, does nothing but burn the hair at the point of contact. As a result it very quickly regrows from that point.

Electrolysis, or diathermy, in the hands of an expert is useful. Here a needle is inserted into the follicle, with the aim of destroying the hair matrix without scarring the skin. Obviously, only a certain number of hairs can be treated at one time, and the procedure is not painless. The problem with this mode of treatment is that too weak a current will not completely dislodge the hair, whereas too strong a current can result in scarring; furthermore, several treatments are usually required to permanently damage the follicle sufficiently to prevent hair regrowth. It is indeed wishful thinking or deceptive advertising to promise single-treatment, permanent hair removal.

HIVES

Hives, known medically as urticaria, are a very common problem. They are sometimes known as 'heat bumps', appearing as raised, red lumps that tend to come and go over any part of the body, and are extremely itchy. They are the result of increased capillary permeability, or 'leaky blood vessels'. The condition has been closely studied by allergists, dermatologists, pharmacologists, and immunologists. As a result the mechanism of action is reasonably well understood. It is thought that various processes, both allergic and non-allergic, lead to the release of certain chemicals, the most important of which is histamine. The histamine is stored in special cells known as mast cells in the connective tissue around the blood vessels. It is here that the antigen-antibody reaction occurs and the histamine and other chemicals are released. These chemicals influence the small blood vessels and capillaries of the skin, leading to skin changes that are characteristic of hives.

There are various known causes of hives (and probably as many unknown).

Foods and additives: Certain foods, including eggs, shellfish, strawberries and nuts, may be implicated. More important, however, are the various food additives, in particular benzoic acid and its derivatives, which are used as preservatives, also the yellow azo dye, tartrazine. A carefully documented dietary chart may help discover whether a particular foodstuff is causing hives. Alternatively, a strict diet may be followed, reintroducing one item at a time. If food preservatives or colouring matter are suspected, then an appropriate diet excluding these may help sort out the problem.

Drugs: Various medications frequently cause hives. These include aspirin and the various salicylates, such as Alka-Seltzer, codeine, Indocid, Brufen, sulphonamides, and of course penicillin may also cause this condition. Some cows are treated with penicillin for mastitis; subsequently, individuals who have a history of penicillin allergy may be absorbing enough penicillin from the milk or other dairy products to cause hives.

Cosmetics, pollens, etc.: Make-up, creams, soaps and shampoos may cause hives, though such cases are rare. Even metal bone prostheses, such as artificial hips or leg plates, may be implicated. Toothpaste containing menthol or fluoride has also been known to cause hives. The inhalation of such things as grass pollens or chromate fumes from welding occasionally causes hives.

Infections: Parasitic infection, in particular various fungi, intestinal worms and hydatids, has frequently been associated with hives. So, also, have viral hepatitis and glandular fever in the presymptomatic stages. Similarly, upper-respiratory-tract infections may be accompanied by hives. Occasionally, bacterial infections such as streptococcal or unsuspected focal dental or sinus infection may cause hives.

Physical causes: Several rarer physical causes of hives exist. For instance, the pressure of belts or shoes may cause localised hives (in this case called pressure urticaria), as may cold air, water or other cold substances. Heat may also cause localised hives if the heat source is local, or generalised urticaria if the condition is provoked by exercise. A still rarer form of hives, solar urticaria, is an allergy to different wave-lengths of ultraviolet light.

Internal disease: Very occasionally, conditions such as lupus erythematosus, leukaemia, or cancer of some organ may cause hives. These can usually be excluded as possible causes by appropriate physical and blood examinations.

Psychological pressure: Emotional stress may either cause or aggravate hives. Whether emotional factors alone can produce these changes is uncertain. Before blaming 'nerves', the various other possible causes must be adequately excluded. Furthermore, treatment should be instituted to relieve the distressing appearance and itch, which only aggravate stress. Adequate explanation and reassurance that the condition is self-limiting must also be given to the patient.

Treatment
The treatment of hives should if possible include identification and removal of the cause. In the absence of any specific cause, the patient must be reassured that there is no apparent allergy or underlying disease. Then symptomatic relief must be instituted.

Unfortunately there are no locally active medications, such as cortisone creams, which have any appreciable effect on hives. Calamine lotion has only a cooling effect. Various drugs are useful, the most commonly used being the anti-histamines. These have varying chemical structures, so if one does not appear to be successful, then another should be tried from a different chemical group. Ephedrine and related drugs may be useful, either alone or with anti-histamines. Hydroxyzine has an ill-understood, but frequently most effective, action on hives. Anti-depressants such as amitriptyline or doxepin, because of their anti-histamine effect, also may have a place in treatment. Finally, if all else fails, oral cortisone may be required in short bursts of low dosage, to help bring the condition under control.

PAPULAR URTICARIA

This is a common condition that mainly affects young children. It is not true urticaria although it resembles hives, but is an exaggerated allergic response to bites. Any biting insect may cause this condition in a susceptible individual. However, fleas, mosquitoes, sand flies, grass mites and bird mites are the commonest. Papular urticaria tends to occur in the spring or summer months, with crops of very itchy lumps, mainly on the limbs. Not each lump is a bite, but rather, an allergic reaction to a bite. The condition is seasonal, reappearing each spring or summer for possibly three or four years before finally disappearing.

Treatment

Treatment entails protecting the child from the relevant insects. This may require the use of mosquito nets, control of fleas on animals, control of lice on birds, and the use of appropriate insect repellants. Topical steroids and antibiotics may be needed if the lumps are infected, as well as anti-histamines.

It has been said that hives lie uneasily between the work areas of the family physician, the dermatologist, the allergist, the physician, and sometimes even the psychiatrist—but in fact they lie just out of the grasp of each of them.

INFECTIONS

The four major types of skin infection are bacterial, viral, fungal and parasitic. These groups will be considered in turn and examples of the most common forms of infection described.

1. BACTERIAL INFECTION

Bacteria live permanently on the skin surface and are known as the permanent bacterial flora. In addition, transient organisms are constantly arriving at the skin surface, but they are usually prevented from multiplying by the normal defence mechanisms. Under certain circumstances either the permanent or transient organisms may become established, multiply excessively, and then cause disease or infection.

The factors governing the host resistance or defence mechanism are several. First, there are the factors inherent in the skin itself; for example, the amount of moisture or other secretions present, and whether there is a point of entry or an abrasion on the surface. Second, there is the degree of interaction between the permanent flora and the invading organism. Finally, there is the factor of the various cellular and circulatory interactions provoked by the invasion: in other words, the degree of resistance or immunity expressed by the body, and the skin in particular.

Impetigo

This a superficial, contagious infection of the skin sometimes known as 'school sores'. As this name suggests, it is most common among school-age children, and appears as spreading sores with honey-coloured crusts. It usually affects more than one person in the family or group, and sometimes seems to be more common in the summer months. Usually it occurs on the face, particularly about the nose and mouth. The common infective organisms are either the staphylococci or streptococci. If untreated, new lesions may continue to erupt for months.

Treatment

Adequate treatment requires the administration of appropriate oral antibiotics. It is not usually sufficient to treat impetigo with applications of antiseptics or antibiotics alone. The only local treatment necessary is the washing of the skin with an antiseptic soap and the gentle lifting off of crusts. Penicillin or erythromycin are usually the most appropriate antibiotics, and will also help prevent possible complications of impetigo such as infection of the kidneys. Recently a powerful new antibiotic ointment, mupirocin, effective against both staphylococci and streptococci, has begun to be used. If you are using this ointment, oral antibiotics are usually not required. Impetigo is very contagious, and affected children should avoid contact with others until healing has occurred.

Boils

Boils are deep infections, usually of hair follicles. They may occur at any age but are more common in adolescents. They can occur at any site except the palms and soles. Friction, such as that often felt in the belt or collar areas, may predispose to their development. Various diseases such as uncontrolled diabetes may aggravate boils, although very few people with boils have, in fact, got diabetes. The most common infective organisms are staphylococci.

Boils may be solitary, multiple, grouped in a cluster—called a carbuncle, or involving an eyelash—called a stye. They are usually red, shiny and very painful swellings.

Treatment

Some boils discharge spontaneously whereas others persist and may cause a severe illness with fever. A single boil may require no treatment other than careful washing with an antiseptic soap, causing it to spontaneously discharge. When there are multiple boils, or if one is in a potentially dangerous site, active treatment is necessary. Initially, a penicillinase-resistant, semi-synthetic penicillin should be administered—cloxacillin, for example. The pus should be cultured, so that the most appropriate antibiotic can then be selected for further treatment.

If boils recur, further investigations are necessary. Cultures should be taken from the infected lesion and from other sites such as the nostrils and genital area. This will identify the reservoir or source of the infective organism. Occasionally cultures taken from other members of the immediate family may be helpful. Appropriate local treatment with an antibiotic cream can then be employed to eradicate the source. Treatment may be assisted by the taking of oral antibiotics and antiseptic baths. Further investigation to exclude possible concurrent diseases such as diabetes, and immunological deficiencies, may occasionally also be necessary.

Other skin infections include *erysipelas* or *cellulitis*, usually caused by streptococci. These infections are deeper than impetigo and may complicate abrasions, surgical wounds or ulcers. Similarly, staphylococci (as in impetigo) often complicate eczema, which may then both mask the diagnosis and complicate the treatment. Many other major bacterial infections affect the skin as well as other organs. These include *tuberculosis, syphilis* and *Hansen's disease* (leprosy).

2. VIRAL INFECTIONS

Viruses are very basic living organisms, consisting of lengths of nucleic acid (either DNA or RNA) and a protective coating, but no cellular structure. They carry enough information for their own replication only but in order to multiply they must use the host's cells, on which they are completely dependent. Anti-viral agents, therefore, often damage the infected cells, although more recent ones tend to be more specific. Viral diseases have now become more of a problem to humans than bacterial infections, because there are only a few safe anti-viral drugs available.

Warts

Warts are a common infection of the skin or mucous membranes. They are caused by the human papilloma virus (HPV), which causes the cells to multiply abnormally, resulting in the growths with which we are so familiar. About fifty-six sub-types of HPV have been identified in the laboratory to date. Different sub-types tend to cause warts at particular sites. As a result we have the common wart, usually quite large and on the fingers; the plane or flat wart, usually on the face or back of the hand; the plantar wart or papilloma, on the sole of the foot; and the genital wart, affecting the ano-genital area.

Warts are transmitted either by direct contact, via infected objects, or autoinoculation from one area to another; but there is no evidence of an association between common and genital warts. Viral particles enter the skin through small abrasions or at sites of trauma or friction. If the area is also moist, infection will be facilitated. Warts occur in all races at all ages, but a peak incidence is around adolescence. The incubation period averages four months but is very variable. The incidence of warts has also increased sharply in the past twenty years, accounting for 10 to 25 per cent of consultations in some UK clinics, compared with 5 per cent previously. Whether warts will develop as a result of inoculation with HPV depends on the amount of virus present and the immune resistance of the individual.

A small number of HPV sub-types are known to cause genital warts, which are highly contagious and usually transmitted sexually. Genital HPV infection in females frequently also involves the cervix, where abnormalities in the cells, known as dysplasia, may result. Most cervical HPV infections clear spontaneously but if dysplasia persists, cancer of the cervix may develop. These changes may be detected on a Pap smear. Consequently, all females who have had genital warts, or whose partners have, are advised to have regular smears.

Treatment

There are many ways of treating warts. This multiplicity indicates that there is no one effective treatment for all warts. In fact warts frequently undergo spontaneous cure, with about 25 per cent resolving within six months; and only a very few survive longer than five years. The aim of treatment should always be to remove the wart without risk to the patient, with minimal pain and no scarring. Effective treatment not only destroys the wart but activates the immune system, which should prevent further infection. The treatment method chosen often depends on the type of wart, the number present, the site and the patient's age.

External applications: The advantage of these applications is that they may be applied by the patient, and are usually inexpensive and relatively painless. They are particularly useful for children and those with large numbers of warts. These preparations may contain salicylic acid, formaldehyde or podophyllin. The latter is particularly useful in the treatment of ano-genital warts, although several treatments may be required and should only be applied by a medical practitioner.

Cryotherapy: Freezing with either carbon dioxide snow (–56.5°C) or liquid nitrogen (–196°C) is a most effective and commonly-used treatment of certain warts. There is also some evidence that recurrent freezing, with the destruction of the host cells, stimulates the immune reaction. Liquid nitrogen is either applied with a cotton bud or sprayed under pressure, but several applications at monthly intervals may be required. The treatment is uncomfortable but does not result in scarring.

Electrodessication and curettage: This method is also known as 'burning out'. It is performed under local anaesthesia, usually on very large and persistent warts. The major disadvantage of this technique is the tendency to scar. It is therefore not recommended for finger warts, where the scar may be unsightly, or plantar warts, where the scar may be more painful than the original wart.

Surgery: Surgical excision is frequently requested in the mistaken belief that if a wart is 'cut out' it will never return. Unfortunately, the rate of recurrence following excision is 25 to 35 per cent. This is thought to be due to the absence of an immune response following the removal of the majority of the viral antigen.

Other more controversial methods: Vitamin A plays a regulatory role in the differentiation of epithelial cells. It has been used both externally and internally with variable success in the treatment of difficult warts. Tretinoin cream is reasonably effective in the treatment of plane warts, and oral Etretinate may also be effective in selected cases.

Cytotoxics such as 5-Fluorouracil in the form of a cream, and Bleomycin as an injection into the wart, have also been used.

DNCB, a chemical to which people develop a severe allergic reaction, has also been used in an attempt to stimulate a person's immunity, so as to enhance the natural rejection process.

These are but a few of the many forms of treatment available for this very common and frustrating viral infection.

Herpes

There are about fifty related herpes viruses. They include those responsible for infectious mononucleosis or 'glandular fever' (Epstein-Barr virus), chicken pox (varicella), cytomegalovirus, fever blisters or 'cold sores' (herpes simplex) and shingles (herpes zoster). The virus is a parasite that invades, reproduces and lives inside the cell and, while it is there, completely disrupts the normal activities of the cell.

Herpes simplex: There are two types of *herpes simplex* virus (HSV)—Type I and Type II. Most people contract Type I, which most often affects the lips, other facial areas and the eye, but may also affect the genital area. Type II usually occurs in the genital area following sexual contact with an infected person.

The initial *HSV I infection* most commonly occurs in childhood from close contact with family members or friends who carry the virus and transmit it to the child by kissing. The initial infection is normally minimal and barely noticeable. The first symptoms of HSV infection may be itchy, tingling and red, sensitive skin. Then tiny fluid-filled blisters appear in varying numbers. When the blisters break, fluid oozes out and scabs form. The process may take ten to fourteen days. However, the virus remains in the body, migrating to nerve cells, where it remains in an inactive state. It may never recur, whereas some people may be plagued with recurrences. Infections seem to be provoked by colds, fever, menstruation, emotional stress and sunlight. Newborn infants and people who are immunosuppressed, due to cancer, drugs, radiotherapy or HIV infection, are prone to severe HSV infections, which may spread internally, and frequently to the brain. HSV

I infections, though common on the lip, may occur on any part of the skin or mucous membranes.

HSV II infections most commonly occur in the ano-genital region of both sexes. Millions of people suffer with this infection. In fact, about 20 per cent of sexually-active adults in the USA are affected, with an estimated half a million new cases appearing each year. Currently it is the most common sexually-transmitted disease. This is no doubt due to increased sexual freedom, young adults' increased mobility, and the popularity of oral contraception. Now, however, following the HIV epidemic, more 'safe sex' using condoms is being practised. Condoms are effective barriers to the HSV and I expect the incidence of this disease to gradually decline.

The initial infection is usually found on the buttocks, penis, vagina or cervix. It occurs two to twenty days after contact with the HSV. While sexual intercourse is the most frequent means of transmission, infection may occur in its absence. The blisters may be accompanied by pain, fever, tender lymph glands and sore muscles. After the initial attack the virus becomes latent in nerve cells. Here it may again be provoked by menstruation, fever, physical contacts, sexual intercourse and sun exposure! Pain is not transmitted from the cervix, so that infection here may go unnoticed. However, like HPV infections, HSV II infection of the cervix is thought to predispose to cancer of the cervix in time. Cervical changes may be detected by regular Pap smears.

Active HSV II infection of the cervix or vagina at childbirth is likely to cause a severe infection in the newborn. To avoid this, Caesarean section is usually performed in these cases. Recurrent HSV II infections tend to become fewer over time and eventually 'burn themselves out'.

Treatment

Most recurrent HSV infections heal spontaneously. Bathing with salt water, keeping the area dry, wearing loose underwear, and taking aspirin, may be all that is required. Further measures may include the application of povidone-iodine paint, wet tea bags (tannic acid) or a local anaesthetic (lignocaine) cream. More specific local treatment is with either idoxuridine, which must be applied frequently and very early, or with acyclovir.

Acyclovir is a new anti-viral drug, effective against members of the herpes group of DNA viruses. This drug appears to shorten the duration of HSV II infection, lessen the severity, and decrease the frequency of recurrences. It is available in an intravenous form, as oral tablets and eye ointment, and skin cream (not in Australia). Internally, it is mainly used for extremely severe primary infections, very frequent and severe recurrences, or in immuno-suppressed patients who are at risk of widespread and possibly fatal disease, and HSV encephalitis. This very useful drug should not be used for trivial infections, so as to minimise the risk of resistant strains of virus developing. Unfortunately, acyclovir cannot eliminate the virus from the body and so provide a cure for this distressing condition.

Herpes zoster: Herpes zoster, or shingles, is a viral infection involving a nerve and the skin overlying it. It is caused by the chicken pox virus (varicella) and is not related to herpes simplex. After a person has been infected with chicken pox, the virus may move to nerves and remain inactive for decades. In the future it may reactivate and cause herpes zoster. Between 10 and 20 per cent of people may develop herpes zoster during their lifetime. It is more common in the elderly, although many more people under the age of 50 are now developing it. Particularly in the younger age group, predisposing conditions must be excluded. These may be internal cortisone treatment, radiotherapy, chemotherapy, leukaemia, Hodgkin's disease, or AIDS.

Herpes zoster is characterised by small, grouped blisters, on a red background, that tend to follow the course of a nerve. The infection will only involve one side of the body, and is associated with itching initially, followed by burning and then pain. Usually it lasts for two to four weeks, with resultant scarring. The most common complication is post-herpetic neuralgia, which is pain that lasts for months or years after the attack has cleared. This occurs in about 10 per cent of elderly patients, but usually resolves within twelve months.

Treatment

The treatment of herpes zoster is primarily of the symptoms. Locally one can use soothing compresses or calamine lotion and orally, simple analgesics. Occasionally, good results are obtained with large doses of oral cortisone that are reduced rapidly over a few days. This is only useful if the treatment is commenced very early in the attack. Acyclovir, the new anti-viral drug—also effective against herpes simplex infection—may also be used, particularly in the elderly and immunosuppressed. It may be given orally or intravenously.

Post-herpetic neuralgia is sometimes very difficult to manage. Various combinations of anti-depressants and anticonvulsants may be helpful. Local anaesthetic sprays, transcutaneous electrical nerve stimulation (TENS) and, more recently, Capsaican has been used. This cream diminishes the pain neuro-transmitter chemical and this may be helpful in some cases.

Pityriasis rosea: This is a common, harmless, non-contagious rash, which is usually without symptoms. It can occur at any age, although it is more common in young adults. A viral cause is suspected although none has yet been isolated.

The condition begins with a single, large, pink scaly patch, usually on the trunk. Within a week or two many similar but smaller patches will appear on the trunk and possibly the upper arms and legs, but never the face. It has a characteristic tree-like pattern on the back, and is rarely itchy. The rash usually fades and disappears within six weeks, without scarring. There is no effective treatment, and the condition does not recur.

3. FUNGAL INFECTIONS

Fungi are living organisms made up of chains of cells, called hyphae, which grow and become intertwined and matted, forming mycelia and spores. In everyday life they can be seen as the mould on old fruit or cheese. There are between 50 000 and 100 000 known species throughout the plant and animal kingdom. Some are useful and productive, such as those that are used to produce penicillin and the antifungal antibiotic, griseofulvin. Relatively few cause problems for humans. Those that do, however, affect many millions of people. It is estimated that fifteen million individuals throughout the world have ringworm of the scalp!

There are two broad categories of fungal infection— dermatophytes and yeasts. When they invade the skin the former cause tinea and the latter thrush.

Dermatophytes

Tinea is usually acquired either through contact with soil, other infected people, or animals. The fungi which cause tinea are called dermatophytes. There are three species of these: Microsporum, which rarely affects the nails; Epidermophyton, which rarely affects hair, and Trichophyton. All of them, however, may affect the epidermis of the skin. Some species are almost solely confined to humans, and these cause milder but more persistent infections than do some other species. Those species that normally infect animals cause a more severe but less prolonged infection when contracted by humans. Some species normally found in the soil may cause tinea in either animals or humans.

Tinea capitis (scalp ringworm) is almost entirely a disease of children, and is mainly transmitted from cats and dogs or from other children. With this disease the appearance of the scalp is one of well-defined round areas of inflammation, scaling and hair loss. The condition is most easily diagnosed by fluorescence of the infected hair shaft when it is placed under a special ultra-violet light, or by examination under the microscope.

Tinea corporis (body ringworm) occurs at all ages and in all races, though it is more common in warm, humid climates. It may be acquired from infected animals and humans, or from infection of the patient's own nails and feet. The classical 'ringworm' begins as a red pimple which enlarges peripherally, with relative clearing centrally. The border is raised, red and well defined. Frequently, it may be confused with discoid eczema. Unfortunately the appearances are not always classical and tinea may occur with many bizarre features. The diagnosis is made either on direct examination of affected skin under the microscope or on cultures of the scrapings. Infected skin does not, unfortunately, fluoresce under the special ultra-violet lamp.

Tinea cruris (Dhobie itch) fungal infections of the groin are more common in men than in women. Tinea cruris is predominantly a summer disease aggravated by the wearing of tight occlusive clothing, particularly nylon. Transmission by towels and other objects may occur, particularly in saunas and communal showers. Cross-infection from the feet is also common. The infection usually begins on the upper inner thigh, with a well-defined border which gradually extends outwards. It is commonly itchy, but rarely ever involves the scrotum.

Tinea pedis (athlete's foot) is a common problem, but the mechanism of transmission is ill understood. Although this disease is more common in hot, humid climates, it virtually only affects people who wear shoes—it is rare, for example, amongst barefooted native peoples. The fungus is thought to be acquired by walking barefoot on fragments of infected skin or nail, particularly around swimming pools or in communal showers. It is uncommon in women, and very rare in children. Children with eczema of the toes are frequently thought, incorrectly, to suffer from tinea because the appearances are similar.

This infection may have symptoms of softening and cracking of the skin between the toes. It may also appear as blisters, or a diffuse scaling on the soles of the feet. It is very rare on top of the foot.

Tinea of the nails is almost always confined to adults, and is usually caused by the same fungus that affects the skin. The earliest change is usually a small area of white, yellow or brown discolouration on one side of the nail, close to the cuticle. This discolouration spreads, and may involve the whole nail. Keratin tissue may build up under the nail and lift it from its bed. The nail may also crumble away, or become thick and distorted. These changes may be easily confused with either paronychia, which is a yeast and bacterial infection of the nailfold, or psoriasis, which has similar features but is not an infection.

Other fungi are able to infect not only the skin and subcutaneous tissue, but internal organs as well. The commonest of these infections are sporotrichosis, chromoblastomycosis, cryptococcosis and histoplasmosis. These conditions are fortunately not common in temperate climates, for they are very difficult to eradicate.

Treatment

The treatment of all these fungal infections is basically similar. Initially, *local applications* should be tried as they are usually adequate for most cases, except for infections of the scalp and nails. Traditional preparations such as Whitfield's ointment or Castellani's paint still have their place, although they are somewhat messy. Tolnaftate cream or lotion is a better application, but the newer imidazole preparations such as clotrimazoole, econazole and miconazole are much superior. Preparations containing nystatin, clioquinol and amphotericin-B are effective against yeast infections but not tinea.

Oral therapy must be resorted to for the treatment of hair and nails, and for many people with chronic tinea elsewhere. The most common drug used is griseofulvin, which is specific for tinea, although poorly absorbed by mouth. Six weeks of treatment is usually sufficient for most infections, but tinea of the nails requires continuous treatment until the nail has grown out normally. This may take from six months to two years.

Ketoconazole is a very effective alternative drug for those who cannot tolerate griseofulvin, or whose infection is resistant to it. Its advantage is that it has a broad spectrum of action against both fungi and yeasts. However, if taken for prolonged periods it may occasionally affect the liver.

Itraconazole is a newer antifungal drug with a broad spectrum of action but apparently without as many side effects.

Yeasts

Thrush: Various yeast organisms normally inhabit the skin's surface as well as the bowel and vagina, the commonest being *Candida albicans*, which is present in and on all of us. Yeasts are single-celled spores that are extremely opportunistic. That is, they easily infect skin or mucous membranes (linings of the mouth, vagina, anus, etc.) which are diseased or damaged. The infection is commonly called *monilia*, or *thrush*. Napkin rashes, and sweat rashes in the creases, are often complicated by overgrowth of monilia. Broad-spectrum antibiotic treatment may destroy the normal bowel or vaginal bacteria, allowing candida to flourish and so cause thrush. Similarly, certain diseases such as diabetes predispose to thrush, as well as immunodeficiency states induced by, for example, either prolonged oral cortisone or HIV infection.

Treatment

Candida infections of the skin are best treated by nystatin, or clioquinol, or one of the imidazole preparations. If it is suspected that the infection has originated from the bowel or vagina, oral or suppository treatment with nystatin may also be required. Very resistant infections may need oral ketoconazole, but griseofulvin is not effective.

Pityriasis versicolor: This is another common skin infection caused by the yeast *Malassezia furfur*. Once again, this yeast is a normal resident of our skin but under certain circumstances invades the skin surface, causing the infection. The factors that predispose to this change are hot or humid climatic conditions, oily skin, or immunosuppression from drugs or disease. It is more common in young men, particularly after holidays in the tropics.

The initial appearance is that of small pink or brownish patches on the upper trunk. They gradually coalesce and lose their colour completely, leaving unsightly, mottled, pale areas that do not tan. The diagnosis is confirmed by microscopic examination of skin scrapings or bright fluorescence under a special lamp.

Treatment

Treatment may be commenced with simple preparations such as Whitfield's ointment, 20 per cent sodium thiosulphate solution or selenium disulphide shampoo. More resistant cases may require one of the imidazole preparations, or oral ketoconazole. Again, griseofulvin is ineffective against this yeast. Recurrent infection is common because the yeast is always present in small amounts and so, usually, are the predisposing factors. Consequently, maintenance therapy is often necessary.

4. PARASITIC INFECTIONS

A variety of parasites, mainly in the form of insects, are known to infect humans or transmit diseases to humans. The skin may become infested by scabies, or the hair-bearing areas by lice.

Scabies

This is the most common parasitic infection, and is caused by the mite *Sarcoptes scabei*. The mite is less than half a millimetre long, and rarely visible to the naked eye. The female is fertilised by the male on the skin surface and then burrows into the skin, laying eggs on the way. The eggs hatch in four days, and grow to mature mites on the surface ten days later. As the life cycle is completed on the skin, untreated infestations will persist indefinitely. Human scabies has played a modest but not insignificant role in history. Severe infestations have lowered the morale of armies in the field, contributing to some major military defeats. Scabies seems to occur in fifteen-year cycles, although there is always a reservoir of infection in the community.

Scabies is normally transmitted by close personal contact, usually in the warmth of a bed. More rarely, it may be acquired from animals, including pets, on whom it may cause a type of mange. Only a few minutes of direct skin contact is necessary to develop scabies. Young adults, particularly the promiscuous, especially during the summer months, tend to contract scabies, and often other sexually transmitted diseases as well!

Most of the symptoms of scabies are a manifestation of the skin's allergic reaction to the mite and its excretions. With a primary infestation, symptoms may not appear for weeks. However, people who have been previously infected may develop spots and itching within hours. The commonest and most disabling symptom of scabies is an intractable, generalised, unrelenting itch. It is markedly worse at night. The burrows, or tunnels, made by the mite are best seen in the finger webs, on the wrist, breast or penis.

Most of what is seen, though, is due to the allergic reaction, such as hive-like spots, small blisters and scratch marks. Secondary bacterial infection is also common. Confirmation of infestation is by microscopic identification of the mite, its eggs or its droppings, found in one of the burrows.

Treatment

Treatment involves the whole family and all intimate contacts. The whole skin from below the chin must be treated, not just the areas that appear to be involved. After a hot bath and scrub, 25 per cent benzyl benzoate emulsion, or 1 per cent gammabenzene hexachloride, should be applied. Twenty-four hours later this should be repeated, without bathing between times. The clothing and bed linen must then be changed. Normal laundering, or hanging up the clothes for a week, will destroy the remaining parasites. The itch may persist, although not as severe, for a couple of weeks after successful treatment. Sufferers will be tempted to repeat the treatment but this should be resisted, otherwise irritation of the skin will occur.

Scabies is by no means a rare infestation these days. It can be very difficult to diagnose in the well-groomed, well-washed individual who is often, in fact, the sufferer of this complaint.

Lice

Infestations of lice are no longer uncommon either. Lice are flat, gray insects nearly half a centimetre long. The wingless female louse lives for about a month, during which time she lays several hundred eggs—called nits. They hatch in about a week, and are fully grown one week later, living off blood sucked from the skin. There are three species of louse—head, body and pubic varieties.

Head lice (Pediculosis capitis) are most common in children, and transmitted by head-to-head contact and shared combs, brushes or hats. They cause severe itching of the scalp and nits are visible, firmly attached to the hairs.

Body lice (Pediculosis corporis) are uncommon, except in vagrants or neglected persons. The eggs or nits are laid in clothing but the louse feeds on human skin, causing intense itching.

Pubic lice (Pediculosis pubis) are reasonably common and usually called 'crabs'. They infest the pubic skin and hairs, again causing itching. This is a disease of young adults and is transmitted via clothing, towels and sexual intercourse.

Treatment

Treatment of the various lice infestations is by the application of gammabenzene hexachloride, malathion or pyrethrin in the form of a cream, lotion or powder. In the case of head lice, the nits should also be combed out with a fine-toothed comb. Because of scratching, secondary bacterial infections are common and these should also be treated.

NAIL DISORDERS

There are a number of relatively minor disorders of the nails and the surrounding skin. These are fairly common in the community, and for this reason will be discussed. Most of the more major disorders are fortunately less common, so only some of these will be mentioned.

PARONYCHIA

This is the most common nail condition seen in medical practice. It is an infection of the nail-fold caused by bacteria and yeast, and only very rarely by fungi. Most commonly, it affects people whose hands are frequently immersed in water. Women are more often affected than men, and diabetics more often than non-diabetics. It is particularly common among housewives, barmen, cooks and cleaners. The predisposing factor is the loss of cuticle, which has most likely been damaged by constant wetting or manicuring. This allows organisms to enter the exposed space between the nail-fold and the underlying nail. One or several fingers may be involved, but the index and middle fingers of the right hand are the most commonly affected. As a result, the nail-fold becomes red, swollen, and painful. Pus may discharge from beneath, and the nail become discoloured and ridged.

Treatment

Treatment involves keeping the nail dry until the cuticle re-forms and is able to exercise its protective function. This means minimising contact with water, soap, detergents and other irritants—a formidable undertaking for those caring for young children. Loose rubber gloves with cotton linings should be used for all wet work. Unlined rubber gloves should be avoided, as they increase the softening of the skin by making the hands sweat. When getting the hands wet is unavoidable, a drying spirit lotion should be immediately applied to the nail-fold after thorough drying of the hands. Overnight, an antibiotic cream effective against both bacteria and yeast should be applied.

HANGNAILS

Hangnails are splits in the skin along the sides of the nails, resulting in pieces of skin breaking away. They are due either to nail biting or to excessive dryness of the skin. Because dried skin loses its elasticity and tends to crack, the tendency is to pick at it. Often the cause of the dryness is repeated washing and/or inadequate drying of the hands. Protection of the hands, adequate drying, and careful manicuring followed by the application of softening ointments, will help prevent hangnails developing.

BRITTLE NAILS (lamellar dystrophy)

This is a common, cosmetic condition, mainly affecting women. The cause is external, never internal. It is thought to be due mainly to overexposure of the hands to water and detergents. This recurrent wetting and drying results in softening, and eventually splitting, of the nail plate into horizontal layers. It is further aggravated by certain nail polishes, and more so by the solvents in nail-polish removers. No amount of calcium, gelatin or vitamin has any effect on this common condition. Wearing cotton-lined rubber gloves for all wet work, frequent use of a moisturising cream, and not removing nail polish too frequently but rather 'touching up', is the best treatment.

NAIL BITING

Nail biting is an extremely common habit, particularly amongst children. Often several members of the family may be nail biters. The patient is usually somewhat anxious, and the family background may contain elements of insecurity. Usually all fingernails are bitten, frequently right back to where the nail plate separates from the nail-bed. Consequently paronychia, nail deformities, hangnail and warts are very common.

Treatment

Occasionally, the application of foul-tasting paint to the nails may discourage the habit, although it is rarely an effective treatment. Some form of psychotherapy is probably the most useful treatment for adults.

FUNGAL INFECTIONS

Fungal infections of the nail are also a reasonably common problem. Several fungi may be involved, including the common fungus responsible for 'athlete's foot'. Initially the infected nail is merely discoloured at the end, but as the infection spreads, it may become softened, fragile, and later thickened. Eventually the nails will separate and lift off, or become grossly distorted. Most commonly, the toenails are the ones affected. Unfortunately, surface applications are rarely sufficient to remedy the situation, nor is removing the affected nail.

Treatment

The most effective treatment is regular clipping of the nail, plus the taking of specific anti-fungal tablets. Because of a toenail's slow rate of growth, and the necessity to take the medication for the entire growth period of the nail, this treatment may be required for anything from six to eighteen months.

INGROWN TOENAILS

An ingrown toenail forms when the edge of a nail penetrates the adjoining soft tissue. The first symptoms are redness and pain, followed by swelling and a discharge. Secondary infection then frequently occurs. The most common causes of this problem are ill-fitting shoes, nails that have been cut too short, excessive curvature of the nail, and flat feet. The first three of these problems may be avoided by wearing adequately wide and long shoes, as well as by cutting the nails straight across and not too short.

Treatment

Mild cases may be treated with wet dressings and by packing sterile cotton wool under the affected edge of the nail. Antibiotics may also be necessary. Severe cases may require an operation.

CORNS

A corn is a coin-shaped overgrowth of hard skin with a central core. Corns usually occur over bony prominences, such as toe joints, or between the toes. They result from chronic pressure or rubbing for long periods. Poorly fitting shoes are the most common cause, but arthritis, improperly positioned toes or bony spurs may also be involved. Prevention requires shoes to fit properly and, occasionally, mechanical devices to position the toes correctly.

Treatment

The corn may be padded over or gradually pared down. The latter may be done with either a salicylic acid paste or the help of a podiatrist. If there is an underlying bony spur, then an orthopaedic surgeon may have to deal with it.

PSORIASIS

Psoriasis frequently affects the nails, resulting in deformities that may precede all other manifestations of the disease. Although the nails may occasionally be the only part of the body affected, in most cases of psoriasis, the symptoms are much more widespread. Almost all patients with psoriasis find their nails are affected at some time during the course of their disease. This, however, may be quite transient. The characteristic changes are fine, thimble-like pitting, lifting, discolouration, and gross thickening of the nails.

Treatment

Treatment of nail psoriasis is most unsatisfactory. Some cases clear spontaneously, whereas others respond to rather painful cortisone injections into the nail-fold. Psoriasis is dealt with more fully in the next section.

ECZEMA OR DERMATITIS

These conditions affecting the hands often affect the nail as well. The usual symptoms are transverse ridging, coarse pitting, discolouration, and eventually marked deformity of the nail. This will all correct itself once the eczema or dermatitis is controlled.

PSORIASIS

Psoriasis, one of the commonest skin diseases, is also one of the most cosmetically disabling. Although it is very rarely fatal, it produces an immeasurable amount of misery. It affects people mainly at the peak of their working and reproductive lives, and has considerable adverse socio-economic effects on them and their families. The disease has been known for hundreds of years. Many of the diseases referred to in the Bible as leprosy are in fact thought to have been psoriasis.

Psoriasis is a skin condition in which red scaly patches develop on the skin. The areas most commonly affected are the elbows and knees, but the scalp and other areas of the body may also be affected. The main problem with the condition is that it is cosmetically unacceptable, both visually and on account of the scales which are shed from the spots. Fortunately the condition very rarely affects the face, and usually appears mainly on areas covered by clothing.

Approximately 2 per cent of the population are affected by one form or other of this condition. It is a familial disease; that is, it is more common in certain families, although its mode of inheritance is debatable. If one parent is affected, there is estimated to be a 25 per cent chance of immediate members of this family also developing the condition. If two parents are affected, then the likelihood increases to 65 per cent. Fortunately, many generations in a family may escape developing the condition.

A number of factors are known to precipitate the onset or appearance of psoriasis. For instance, certain infections, such as a streptococcal tonsillitis, are known to be implicated, particularly in children. Trauma, due to such things as injuries or sun-burn, may also cause the appearance of psoriasis. It has been suggested that certain hormonal changes, such as those occurring with puberty and menopause, may aggravate the condition; yet certain other hormonal changes, such as those during pregnancy, may improve the disease. As with many other conditions, psychological stress can certainly aggravate the disease. Even some drugs, such as beta blockers for the treatment of hypertension, or lithium for the treatment of depression, may aggravate psoriasis.

Psoriasis has various forms. There is the *acute* or *guttate form* of the condition, which is usually seen in children and may be precipitated by tonsillitis.

Then there is the *chronic* or *plaque form*, which is the commonest manifestation. It classically affects the elbows, the knees, the buttocks and the scalp. In this latter area, it may easily be confused with severe dandruff.

Flexural psoriasis is confined to the creases or flexures, and sometimes in infancy it occurs as a napkin psoriasis. Here it may be confused with a simple napkin dermatitis, or eczema.

Nail psoriasis can be most disfiguring. It may affect the nails only or be associated with other forms of psoriasis. Usually it causes lifting of the nail, with or without pitting, and eventually, disintegration. This condition may be misdiagnosed as a fungal infection, from which it must always be separated, as the treatment is very different.

Most infrequently, psoriasis takes on a *pustular form*, and then is mainly distributed on either the palms or soles, where it has the appearance of an infective process. It is not, however, infective or infectious.

Rarer still is the *exfoliative form* of psoriasis, where the entire body skin is shed, and the patient becomes extremely ill.

Another of the rare complications of psoriasis is an arthritis, which mainly affects the finger or toe joints, and occasionally the cervical spine, or lower back joints. Psoriasis, however, is not contagious, nor does it affect the blood, or cause cancer.

The basic pathology of psoriasis is related to increased reproductivity of the cells in the skin and increased production of DNA in the epidermis and dermis. Certain abnormalities in enzymes, which control cell proliferation, are present in people with psoriasis. There are also abnormalities of immune cells in the skin. How this comes about is as yet uncertain, although much research work is being done in order to try to elucidate the basic fault, in the hope that one day it may be corrected. As a result of these abnormalities in the skin, there is a marked increase in the rate of cell 'turnover'. The abnormal cells reproduce about twelve times more quickly than the normal cells, resulting in a build-up of cells that appears as thick scale.

The treatment of such a disfiguring condition is obviously of considerable importance. A society that extols the virtues of physical beauty as much as ours makes people with psoriasis feel very self-conscious. The question is always asked: 'Can psoriasis be cured?'. Unfortunately it is no more 'curable' than high blood pressure, schizophrenia or diabetes. However—and this must be stressed—in most cases it can be completely controlled so that there may be no evidence of the condition at all for long periods of time. Even though the condition may recur, it can once again be brought under complete control.

Treatment

The overall aim of treatment is to inhibit or reduce the mitotic activity of the cells, so that they slow down their rate of reproduction or 'turnover'. Along with this, the associated inflammation must be suppressed. *Topical or surface treatment* is the most logical form of treatment. The most useful substances for this are tar preparations and a closely-related substance known as dithranol. Both suppress DNA synthesis by interfering with a number of cellular processes, thereby normalising the structure of the epidermis. These preparations may come in various forms, and one of the most important considerations when using these substances is the choice of vehicle; some bases, whether cream or ointment, are better absorbed than others, enabling the tar or dithranol to adequately penetrate the skin. The vehicle is particularly important when the preparation is intended for use on the scalp. If, for example, an ointment were to be used here, it may be difficult to wash out in the morning, and therefore cosmetically unsuitable; ointment, therefore, would not be used. Frequently, these preparations may be used in conjunction with salicylic or retinoic acids, which are very useful in reducing the surface scaliness and allowing the preparations to adequately penetrate the tissues. The reduction in cell turnover, induced by dithranol, is longer lasting than that induced by topical steroids.

Topical steroids, or 'cortisone' creams are very commonly used in the treatment of psoriasis. The advantage of these preparations is, first, that they are cosmetically the most acceptable. Furthermore, they are excellent for decreasing mitoses, decreasing surface scaliness, and reducing inflammation. However, the weaker creams do not work effectively and use of the stronger ones, over large surfaces for prolonged periods, may occasionally result in side effects. The other, perhaps more important, disadvantage is that the condition frequently recurs, or relapses, when the sufferer stops using them. Once again, the base of the preparation affects its potency. Ointments are more effective than creams, and a propylene glycol base provides optimal penetration of the active agent.

Because of its cytotoxic action, 5-Fluorouracil has also been used. This has mainly been of use in localised areas of pustular psoriasis. If used continuously it may cause ulceration.

Nitrogen mustard is also a cytotoxic agent that induces a reduction in cell turnover. It is applied to the skin after dilution with water, but it may be quite toxic and many people become allergic to it.

Phototherapy, such as the beneficial effect of sunlight on psoriasis, has been known for years. Ultraviolet-B (290–320 nm) tends to decrease mitoses and reduce excessive cell reproduction. The sun is the best source, but is not always available. Natural or artificial UVB is a very useful adjunct to the treatment of psoriasis with both tar and dithranol.

More recently, ultraviolet-A (320–400 nm) has been employed, utilising a special cabinet fitted out with tubes emitting this radiation. In conjunction with this a photosensitising drug, known as psoralen, is taken. This drug absorbs the UVA light, intensifying its action on the skin and also having some immunological effect. The treatment is known as PUVA. Treatment is given two to three times per week initially and must be maintained from time to time. PUVA is not a first-line treatment because of its many potential side effects. These include burns, if the dosage is incorrect or if the patient does not protect him or herself from sunlight for twelve hours after treatment. It also may affect certain blood cells, and cause cataracts if special goggles are not worn during and for twelve hours after treatment. More importantly, the treatment has the potential to cause considerable photo-ageing and skin cancer. Unfortunately these cancers are not always the relatively benign basal cell carcinoma; more commonly they are the malignant squamous cell carcinoma, or even melanoma.

Systemic or oral treatment of psoriasis is also available for the more severe cases. This type of treatment should only be carried out by dermatologists who are prepared to carefully monitor the patient's general health and carefully control the dosage of the drugs used. Oral cortisone has no place in the routine management of psoriasis because of its possible side effects with continued use. Furthermore, with acute pustular psoriasis it may aggravate the condition.

Various cytotoxic agents (like methotrexate), which in large doses are used for the treatment of certain cancers, may be most useful when used in low dosage. They act by inhibiting mitoses and slowing down cell reproduction. Methotrexate is used in very small doses that are given once a week. It is a very useful drug if the patient has no blood or liver abnormalities, which must be regularly checked. Obviously methotrexate affects not only the skin but also the liver, bone marrow, bowel and reproductive organs. It must therefore never be used during reproductive years unless appropriate contraceptive precautions are taken. However, if used with care and appropriate supervision, methotrexate is a most useful treatment for severe psoriasis.

There are other similar drugs, such as hydroxyurea, that may be used if methotrexate proves unsatisfactory. Cyclosporine is not a cytotoxic drug, but one which has an immunological effect. It is mainly used to prevent rejection of kidney transplants. However, it has recently been shown to be very effective in quite low doses in the treatment of psoriasis. Currently it is being investigated, but its use is limited by both its cost and its possible toxicity.

Retinoids are synthetic derivatives of vitamin A. Etretinate is the one most effective in the treatment of some forms of psoriasis, particularly pustular psoriasis. It is taken daily, but may have side effects. The major toxic effect is that it causes embryological changes, resulting in birth defects. Consequently, it is rarely given to women of childbearing age, and if it is, adequate contraception must continue for two years after cessation of treatment. This is because the drug may be stored in body fat for that period of time. Cholesterol levels may also be elevated, and some liver enzyme changes can occur.

Another vitamin A derivative, Etretin, is soon to be marketed. It has the advantage of fewer side effects and quicker clearance from the body.

Because psoriasis is a chronic disease, with numerous ups and downs and no definitive cure, doctors and patients alike are tempted to try 'alternative methods', particularly 'natural cures'. These include fish oil, vitamin D, capsaican cream, various diets, salt water baths, and meditation. Many patients attend naturopaths, chiropractors and allergists. It is wise to remember, though, that 30 per cent of patients will have a spontaneous remission at some stage of their illness. On a brighter note, I can assure you that research is progressing, and a better understanding of the disease has resulted in improved treatment methods. If these are used in the appropriate situation they may be very effective. Newer methods, of course, are also on the horizon.

SYPHILIS

Syphilis is capable of producing the most varied of all skin changes. It may also mimic a wide variety of internal diseases. Consequently it is essential to bear in mind the possibility of any unusual rash being due to syphilis.

Syphilis is a chronic infectious disease caused by the bacillus *Treponema pallidum*, which is acquired by intimate contact with an infected person or as a congenital infection in infancy. In the Western world it is most easily transmitted, under moist conditions, by genital or oral contact. It may also be transmitted by an infected mother from the fifth month of pregnancy onwards. In underdeveloped countries a form of syphilis occurs which is spread by intimate contact rather than by sexual intercourse; it is usually associated with bad living conditions and poor hygiene.

In Europe until recently from 30 000 to 40 000 cases of contagious syphilis were registered every year, the greatest incidence being amongst homosexual men. As with all venereal diseases, syphilis is more common during times of unstable social conditions and war. After World War II cases rapidly declined. However the past twenty years has seen a marked resurgence. The reasons for this are speculative but may include: increased travel, both tourist and migratory; altered moral standards; a more liberal attitude to homosexuality; the effect of oral and intrauterine contraceptives on human sexual behaviour; the diminished use of condoms, and the widespread use of drugs. However, since the advent of HIV infection and the subsequent tendency to practise 'safe sex', particularly among homosexuals, the incidence of syphilis is gradually declining.

Syphilis may be thought of as occurring in four stages. *Primary infection* occurs ten to thirty days after contact, and takes the form of a persistent chancre or sore. Associated with this there are enlarged tender lymph glands. The chancre usually appears on the genitals, in the anal area, or in or around the mouth. It may take three to eight weeks to heal, leaving a small scar. At this stage, it is best diagnosed by a direct bacterial examination of the sore.

Secondary syphilis will usually occur one to two months after the primary stage. This stage may manifest a wide variety of different rashes, and is best diagnosed by appropriate blood tests. At this time the person is highly contagious, and bacteria may be found on most parts of the body. This stage may persist for up to two years. The rashes may resemble measles, chicken pox, hives, drug allergies, tinea, eczema, warts and psoriasis, to name but a few conditions. However, invariably there are other associated symptoms, such as a fever, tiredness, patchy hair loss, joint pains and headaches, particularly at night. This stage is also accompanied by enlarged, but not tender, lymph glands.

Latent syphilis, which is the stage without symptoms, may last from two to twenty years. It is only diagnosed from an adequate history and positive blood tests.

The final stage, *tertiary syphilis*, may affect all organs of the body; more commonly, though, it affects the heart, brain and liver. In the skin it appears either as odd patterns of grouped nodules or large, painless ulcers. This stage is not infectious.

Treatment

The treatment for syphilis is penicillin. For primary and secondary stages, this is either given on ten consecutive days or in one very large single dose. Syphilis sufferers require follow-up treatment, including blood tests for two years. Contact tracing of people who are likely to have become infected is an essential part of the proper management of this contagious and important disease. Cases of syphilis that are of longer than twelve months' duration require more intensive therapy over a longer period.

ZOONOSES

These are diseases which are acquired from animals. A variety of animals—both domestic and others—are known to transmit diseases to man. A number of these diseases are described below.

Several *bacterial infections* which affect humans may be contracted from animals. Domestic dogs and cats, being the most popular of household pets, are especially likely to be implicated in this regard. Both staphylococcal and streptococcal germs are carried in the mouths and throats of dogs and cats, and are easily transmitted to their owners. As well as transmitting their own infections to humans, pets may also convey infections they themselves have acquired from people, back to humans.

Brucellosis is a bacterial infection of cattle, sheep, goats and pigs. This may be contracted by humans, either through contact with infectious milk or directly from the infected animals. In addition to skin infections, brucellosis may cause a high fever and muscle pain. Another bacterial disease, anthrax, is contracted from the handling of infected bones, hides, wool or hair of animals. The disease may cause severe pustular infections, associated with very high fever, and may be fatal. Cat-scratch disease, which usually results in painful, enlarged lymph glands and rashes, may be contracted as a result of being scratched by an infected cat or kitten. Tropical fish enthusiasts are not immune from infection either. The water in tropical fish tanks is often contaminated by the bacteria mycobacterium marinum, which closely resembles the tuberculosis germ. It may also be present in lakes, spas or heated swimming pools. Infection usually occurs at the site of an abrasion. It appears as a lump or infection, which breaks down to form a non-healing sore. Most commonly, it occurs on the hands. Treatment with the appropriate antibiotic is usually satisfactory.

Similarly, there are a number of *viral infections* of animals which may affect humans. These include ornithosis, a most unpleasant disease which may affect the lungs, heart or liver, and cause a fever and a fairly characteristic rash. This disease may be contracted from over 120 species of birds, including pigeons, domestic fowl, ducks, parrots, and even finches. Human infections occur from the inhalation of infected dust from excreta or feathers. Another viral infection, foot-and-mouth disease, is common in European and Asian farm animals. Rarely, however, does it infect humans. When it does, it results in blisters of the mouth, tongue, lips and the palms and soles. It tends to be more severe in infants and children than adults. The disease milkers' nodule is derived from the teats of infected cows, and results in tender, red lumps on the fingers of those who milk these cows. Orf is a similar condition, mainly derived from lambs. It infects humans, either through their direct contact with the affected animal, dead or alive, or even through contact with contaminated pastures. It results in painful nodules on the hands which may ulcerate.

Animals are also known to transmit a number of *fungal infections* to man. Four of these infections are frequently causes of ringworm; they are: microsporum canis, commonly found on cats and dogs; trichophyton verrucosum, commonly found on cattle; trichophyton mentagrophytes and microsporum gypseum, soil inhabitants. (Ringworm is discussed in detail elsewhere.) There are other fungal infections which not only infect the skin but the internal organs as well. Fortunately—for they are difficult to treat—such infections are rare. In Australia there are three forms which are known to affect man: sporotrichosis, blastomycosis and cryptococcosis.

Certain *parasites* harboured by our pets may be transmitted to us accidentally. These parasites may be a source of irritation in themselves, or they may be carriers of some disease. One of the more serious of these parasite-transmitted diseases is hydatids. Normally, the tapeworm responsible for the disease lives in the intestine of the dog, and if its eggs are accidentally swallowed by man, large hydatid cysts develop internally. The common intermediate host is the sheep, which may eat infected grass. However, humans can also contract the disease by eating infected sheep, although this is uncommon. Other parasitic worms which may affect humans are cat or dog hookworms. These may be picked up from infested soil, the worms depositing larvae which are able to penetrate the skin. This results in a characteristic creeping eruption. Similarly, swimmer's itch is caused by penetration of the skin by the larvae of bird worms. This is usually picked up in shallow lakes from snails, which are the intermediate hosts. Another infection, leptospirosis, is an infection caused by a parasite frequently found in domestic animals (including dogs, pigs and cattle) and rats. Humans are usually infected by contact with infected urine via a cut or an abrasion. The resultant illness may be experienced as a mixture of fever, muscle pain, rashes, headaches and jaundice.

There are a number of other quite common external animal parasites, mainly of dogs and cats, which not infrequently affect humans. One of these is mites, of which there are a number of species. One species, *sarcoptes scabiei*, may cause a form of mange in dogs, cats, rabbits and foxes. The mites are spread by direct, intimate contact, either with affected pets or more commonly, affected people! Only a few minutes of direct contact is necessary to develop scabies. The mites burrow under the skin, mate and lay their eggs. Their burrows are mainly found on the hands, wrists and genital area. The mites are quite prolific breeders, and the body quickly builds up an allergic reaction to these foreign invaders. This is usually manifest as an intense itch. The itching is worse at night, when the body is warm, and the mites and larvae perambulate in this cosy atmosphere.

There are over 1000 species of fleas, small, wingless parasites that live on some animals—dogs, cats, rabbits—and some birds.

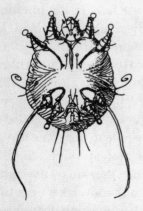

THE SCABIES MITE
(Sarcoptes scabiei)

THE BODY LOUSE
(Pediculus humanus corporis)

Fleas will, in the absence of their usual host, feed on humans. Some people have specific allergic reactions to their bites; some people also seem to be more attractive to fleas than others! As fleas may be the vectors of typhus, bubonic plague and tularaemia, their control is very much in the interests of public health. Lice infections are no longer uncommon. Lice may be transmitted to human by animals although this, in fact, happens fairly rarely.

Various mites which infest animals or birds may infect humans. These may either cause a severe disease, such as Scrub Typhus which is transmitted by rats, or an allergic response known as *papular urticaria.*

Some individuals may be allergic to dogs' or cats' saliva, and may develop swellings and allergic eczema if licked by these animals. Other allergic manifestations such as asthma and hay fever may also develop. Hypersensitivity amongst humans to bird feathers and eggs is not rare, and may cause asthmatic attacks, hives or hay fever.

Index

A

acne, types of, 134
acne, treatment of, 136
acne, 18, 51, 133, 134, 135, 103, 140, 144
acne, variants of, 140
acne surgery, 139
acne scarring, 69
adolescence, 9, 19, 135, 140
age spots, 54, 73
AIDS, 141, 144, 178
alcohol, 2, 20, 23, 94, 98
allergies, 98, 115, 145
alopecia, 81, 85, 160–161
animals, 197
anti-histamines, 101, 156, 170
anti-depressants, 100–101
arthritis, 191
asthma, 152, 200
athlete's foot, 181

B

bacterial infections, 144
baldness, 161–162, 165
baldness, treatment of, 162
beauty marks, 127
beauty spots, 75

benign growths, 72
birthmarks, 15, 18, 75, 77
blackheads, 51, 56, 134
boils, 172, 173
broken capillaries, 53, 56, 74

C

Candida albicans, 143, 182
carcinoma, 119–121
chicken pox, 143
    see also herpes zoster
chronological ageing, 54, 55
cleansing, 2, 21, 23
cold sores, 142, 157
    see also herpes simplex
collagen, 7, 13, 48, 50, 54–55, 57, 63
collagen implants, 26, 69, 70, 71, 139
corns, 189
corticosteriod, 99, 101–105, 155, 159, 165
cortisone, 101, 156
cosmetics, 20, 39, 43, 47, 148
cosmetics industry, 40, 44
cradle cap, 159
cryotherapy, 116, 175